New Horizons

TEACHER'S BOOK

4

Paul Radley   Daniela Simons
Rónán McGuinness

Contents

Great Clarendon Street, Oxford, OX2 6DP, United Kingdom

Oxford University Press is a department of the University of Oxford.
It furthers the University's objective of excellence in research, scholarship,
and education by publishing worldwide. Oxford is a registered trade
mark of Oxford University Press in the UK and in certain other countries

ISBN: 978 0 19 413468 2

Printed in China

This book is printed on paper from certified and well-managed sources

ACKNOWLEDGEMENTS

*The authors and publisher would like to thank Barbara Csiszár, Daniel Nolan and
Rézműves László for their contributions to the development of this Teacher's Book.*

Introduction

New Horizons is a four-level course developed for students working towards their B1 school-leaving exam. *New Horizons* is modern and communicative, and sets achievable goals with material presented in a user-friendly format. The course caters for a range of teaching scenarios with different entry points, depending on the starting level of the class.

New Horizons has a clear and accessible approach. Grammar points are clearly presented and thoroughly practised, and vocabulary is presented and recycled to give students the confidence they need to use and extend what they have learned. Skills are developed systematically, with particular attention being paid to developing speaking skills through a variety of pair and group activities.

Skills and culture sections at the end of each unit develop all four language skills through typical exam task types throughout the series.

Exam plus lessons in the *Student's Book* systematically cover all the key exam topic areas, developing vocabulary as well as all the exam skills necessary to complete the exam successfully. The accompanying exam reference sections (*Writing bank* in the *Student's Book* and *Functions bank* in the *Workbook*) provide students with comprehensive exam preparation solutions, integrated into the *New Horizons* course.

The course material is presented through realistic stories and scenarios set in the UK. The story involves characters from English-speaking countries around the world who come to England to take part in a journalism competition. The context of all the *Student's Book* units is that of everyday life for teenagers, and material in the *Skills and culture* sections introduces different aspects of life in Britain, the USA, India and New Zealand, as well as topics with a European emphasis. Through this presentation of culture that is both interesting and relevant to their own experience, students can draw parallels and discover differences that will lead to a greater understanding of the English language and the global culture that informs it.

New Horizons: flexible teaching and learning

New Horizons is designed to offer flexibility both in terms of starting levels and of number of weekly contact hours.

The course is designed to allow for variations in allocated class time and term structure. The core *Student's Book* material can be covered in a relatively low number of weekly lessons. The course is divided into four levels (beginner to intermediate) to take students from level A1 of the Common European Framework, and aiming towards level B1+ by the end of the course.

New Horizons and exams

Students preparing for exams need a clear, achievable learning structure, reliable guidance and thorough, focused practice for the exam they will face at the end of their studies. Throughout the course, *New Horizons* builds students' abilities and confidence, providing them with the support they need.

New Horizons covers the grammatical and lexical syllabus typically required by B1 exams and enables students to express themselves appropriately over a full range of exam topics. The course features systematic exam preparation, right from the beginning, with characteristic exam task types in the *Skills and culture* sections. Exam tips and Study Strategies provide the students with structured guidance and useful strategies for dealing with all the task types they will face. As the course progresses, so the exam preparation develops, providing students with the platform from which to succeed in their exam.

As the coursebook series approaches the end of secondary studies, there is an increased emphasis on effective exam preparation in *New Horizons 3* and *4*. Four *Exam plus* sections linked to the topics of the main units – as well covering a wide range of exam topic requirements – provide material for intensive exam preparation. These lessons develop the skills to tackle every key exam task type, building up students' awareness of exam expectations and assessment criteria, as well as strategies and techniques for preparation for and successful completion of these tasks. By the end of *New Horizons 4*, students should be ready to take the exam at the B1 level.

There are also four dedicated exam practice sections in the *Workbook*, providing material for Reading, Listening, Use of English, Writing and Speaking tasks. The audio material for these *Workbook* sections is recorded on the MultiROM disc at the back of the *Student's Book*.

Comprehensive reference banks in the *Student's Book/ Workbook* provide background information as well as exam self-study material with a *Writing bank* (featuring model texts and useful advice for typical Writing exam tasks), and a *Functions bank* (a collection of useful phrases for every communicative situation students are likely to encounter in the oral exam).

New Horizons and evaluation

The term *evaluation* should be taken to mean a complex system including continual assessment, self-assessment, testing and external exams. By making use of all of these evaluation strategies teachers can obtain a full picture of the student, concentrating not just on the final product (the grade) but above all on the learning process itself. The assessment, therefore, must be constructive: on the one hand focusing on the student's successes (i.e. how much he/she knows) rather than on his/her failures; and on the other, directing him/her towards areas needing revision or consolidation. For continuous feedback on the students' learning process, testing and assessment must be based on:

- **Informal assessment** – during the learning process,
- **Self-assessment** – diagnostic self-assessment at regular intervals encouraging students to think about their own learning process,
- **Formal assessment** – at established intervals and for different purposes (e.g. diagnostic, progress or achievement tests).

Informal assessment

Continuous assessment is a way of keeping students' progress in view and focusing on their general ability, when the pressure of exams is not a factor. Choose a skill for assessment, or a number of students in a group to focus on, and make a note of their performance in a given lesson. Whether you tell them you will be doing this is up to you. Use your observations to inform feedback to students and to compare with their own assessment of their competence and progress.

Self-assessment

Self-assessment plays an important part in the learning process. It involves students consciously in their study of the language, as it pushes them to reflect upon and evaluate their own ability and to develop plans and strategies for improving on strengths and addressing weaknesses. New Horizons deals with this important question through:

- Grammar checks in every unit to provide an interactive grammar summary.
- Language review sections after every two units to reflect on the language and functional skills students have learned and the progress they have made.
- Photocopiable Stop and check tables at the back of the Teacher's Book enable students to check their progress against the descriptors of the Common European Framework of Reference.

Formal assessment

Formal assessment serves various purposes: it can be used as a diagnostic tool to identify strengths and weaknesses of groups or individual students; it can provide feedback on the whole or the components of the teaching syllabus; or it can form the basis of marks or grades given to students. At the beginning of the school year or the course, it can also assist teachers in making decisions about placement of students in groups according to their level of English.

Teachers can select from a large variety of forms of assessment:

- checking students' written or oral homework,
- asking students to perform communicative or lexical tasks in class,
- short quick tests to assess a particular skill or language point,
- longer progress tests (either provided with the coursebook they are using, or designed by the teachers themselves).

New Horizons provides photocopiable progress tests on a separately available Teacher's Resource CD, which are designed to be used after completing each unit. For each unit, there are two alternative tests (Groups A and B) to eliminate cheating and to offer flexibility.

New Horizons and culture

Learning a foreign language is a far more complex process than simply learning rules or skills, a process which necessarily involves empathy towards a foreign culture and its behaviour and lifestyle.

A language course focusing on the student as a whole person must aim to broaden their cultural horizons and help them to get around confidently and independently in a situation where use of the foreign language is necessary. For just this reason, foreign language teaching can bring to life intercultural education.

New Horizons guides the student along this linguistic and cultural path. It involves the student in a series of stories whose main characters are young people from various English-speaking countries such as the UK, India, the USA and New Zealand. In this way the student is invited into an international and multicultural environment, where they are introduced to subjects ranging from the day-to-day life of teenagers, to the wider social and cultural questions surrounding them.

New Horizons and the Common European Framework of Reference

New Horizons was developed in line with the Council of Europe's Common European Framework of Reference. This allows students and teachers to evaluate their progress against a set of standard European specifications. Teachers and students will find reference to the CEFR descriptors in the photocopiable Stop and check pages at the back of the Teacher's Books. These sections encourage regular self-assessment and conscious focus on progress. With the teacher's help, students can identify weaknesses and set goals within an individual learning strategy.

New Horizons methodology

New Horizons is a modern, reliable course that sets achievable goals by encouraging learner autonomy while providing ample teacher support and a clear, easily teachable structure.

New Horizons employs a communicative methodological approach. Particular attention has been paid to developing speaking skills and constant opportunities are given for students to use the language they have acquired in the context of real communication, whether individually, in pairs, or in groups.

The course encourages systematic teaching based on constant practice following the pattern of:

1 presentation
2 controlled practice
3 semi-controlled practice
4 free practice
5 open communication
6 testing and self-assessment

Each unit is clearly organised and follows the same pattern. The aim of the six pages of presentation and practice is to give students communicative competence to encourage confident use of the language they have acquired. Grammar is practised systematically and vocabulary is acquired gradually and continually recycled. In the double-page Skills and culture sections at the end of every unit all four skills are practised systematically.

New Horizons characteristics

- Very clear structure: traditional methodology with up-to-date content that appeals to teenage learners as well as to teachers.

- Current issues and topics as well as more serious, educational themes.
- Compatibility with the Common European Framework of Reference – covering levels A1 to B1+.
- International and multicultural dimensions – the book's recurring characters are teenagers from several English-speaking countries around the world.
- Authentic English – presentation of idiomatic phrases and current vocabulary (*Learn it! Use it! Translate it!*).
- Systematic and cohesive study of grammar, functions and vocabulary.
- Regular reflection on grammar – accompanied by exercises at the end of every unit to check that the main structures have been assimilated.
- Integrated skills development – all four skills are practised in every unit through activities which always reflect the grammatical content and theme of the unit.
- Dedicated intensive exam training – key exam topics and tasks are covered in the *Exam plus* sections.

Components

- *Student's Book* with interactive MultiROM giving access to a free practice exam online at www.oxfordenglishtesting.com
- *Workbook*
- iTools (for use with interactive whiteboards and/or personal computers)
- *Teacher's Book*
- Class audio CDs
- Teacher's Tests CD
- teacher's website (with downloadable classroom materials)
- student's website (with interactive self-study activities)

How the course is organised

Student's Book

The *Student's Book* comprises:
- eight units covering the core syllabus,
- four *Language review* lessons, one after every two units,
- eight *Exam plus* pages, linked to the main units of the book but designed to use flexibly for intensive exam preparation,
- eight *Language plus* lessons, revising and extending each main unit,
- a *Writing bank* with model texts and advice.

Workbook

The *Workbook* comprises:
- a variety of exercises mirroring the language and topics in the *Student's Book*, which features specific recommendations for extra practice or homework tasks in each lesson,
- translation exercises addressing particular points of difficulty,
- interesting cultural facts (*Did you know…?*),
- a comprehensive Grammar reference section,

- a complete wordlist containing all the active vocabulary from each *Student's Book* unit,
- a *Functions bank* with useful phrases for communicative situations.

iTools

Presentation and practice software materials for the digital classroom including:
- audio-visual materials,
- answer keys and highlighted tapescripts,
- additional CLIL worksheets,
- user's guide with each package.

Teacher's Book

The *Teacher's Book* includes:
- introduction,
- teaching notes and answer key for the *Student's Book* exercises,
- *Workbook* answer key,
- transcripts of recorded audio material,
- suggestions for optional supplementary activities,
- culture and language notes.

Class CDs

Each level of the course is accompanied by a double set of class CDs featuring the recorded audio material for all of the listening exercises. The audio material reflects the multi-cultural nature of the course and includes a variety of accents.

Tests

Tests for *New Horizons* are provided on a Teacher's Tests CD and consist of:
- progress tests – in Group A and Group B versions, designed for use after completing each unit,
- short tests – 10-minute tests of grammar and vocabulary for spot checks of comprehension of key language.

Websites

The *New Horizons* teacher's website is part of the OUP Teachers' Club at www.oup.com/elt/teachersclub. You need to register to use this free service, offering reference and downloadable classroom materials.

The *New Horizons* student's website can be found at www.oup.com/elt/newhorizonscee. Students can access interactive activities and games free of charge.

	Topic and vocabulary	Grammar	Functions	
THE STORY SO FAR / QUICK CHECK p.4				
UNIT 1 p.6	Exercise and fitness Past habits Skills and ability Extreme sports New Zealand	*used to* • past habits Formation and comparison of adverbs Verbs with *to*-infinitive or *-ing*	Talking about past habits Comparing ability Talking about lifestyles	
UNIT 2 p.16	The body Appearance Advice Health, illnesses, remedies Body image	*have/get* something *done* *should, ought to*	Getting things done Giving advice Talking about health	
UNIT 3 p.26	Emotions Wishes Feelings TV reality shows Mind games	Second conditional *wish* + Past simple *make* + object + adjective/verb	Imagining different situations Making wishes Talking about feelings	
UNIT 4 p.36	The European Union Relationships Dating customs in the past and present	Question tags Past perfect Phrasal verbs Reported speech • *say, tell*	Checking information Describing events Reporting statements	
UNIT 5 p.46	Crime and punishment Requests Addictions Mistakes in life	*should have, ought to have* Reported speech • *ask, tell, want*	Talking about past mistakes Reporting questions Reporting requests and instructions	
UNIT 6 p.56	Charities and world problems The news Soccer Aid Raising money for charity	Past simple passive Present perfect passive Present continuous passive Future passive Reflexive and reciprocal pronouns	Talking about past facts Talking about developments	
UNIT 7 p.66	Relationships Texting Technology	Phrasal verbs Questions revision • different tenses *be/get used to* Verb tense revision	Asking questions Talking about familiar things	
UNIT 8 p.76	Life choices Regrets Shopping Consumerist society	Third conditional Conditionals revision *wish* + Past perfect	Imagining a different past Talking about regrets	

Language plus 1–8 pp.86–101   **Writing bank** pp.102–107   **Resources** pp.108 & 111

Skills and pronunciation	Optional extension	
Reading: matching headings, multiple-choice gap-fill (*magazine article, country factfile*) **Listening**: multiple-choice questions (*radio show*) **Speaking**: quiz questions (*films and actors*) **Writing**: a paragraph (*your favourite actor*) **Pronunciation**: *used to*	Language plus 1 p.86 Exam plus • p.14	LANGUAGE REVIEW UNITS 1 & 2 p.24
Speaking: conversation (*body image*) **Reading**: predicting content, comprehension questions (*magazine article*) **Listening**: true or false (*interview*) **Writing**: email (*giving advice*) **Pronunciation**: vowel sounds	Language plus 2 p.88 Exam plus • p.15	
Speaking: conversation (*mind games*) **Reading**: predicting content, matching photos to information, true or false (*magazine article*) **Listening**: listening for general understanding, multiple matching (*discussion*) **Writing**: a summary (*summarising an article*) **Pronunciation**: *you* + vowel sound	Language plus 3 p.90 Exam plus • p.34	LANGUAGE REVIEW UNITS 3 & 4 p.44
Listening: comprehension questions (*interview with a married couple*) **Speaking**: discussing facts (*dating customs*) **Reading and speaking**: jigsaw reading/information gap, asking and answering questions, group discussion of advantages and disadvantages (*magazine article, a personal profile*) **Writing**: a personal profile **Pronunciation**: intonation	Language plus 4 p.92 Exam plus • p.35	
Speaking: discussing opinions, reflecting on the article (*drug addiction*) **Reading**: predicting content, comprehension questions (*magazine article*) **Listening**: true or false (*interview*) **Writing**: a story (*mistakes in life*) **Pronunciation**: silent consonants	Language plus 5 p.94 Exam plus • p.54	LANGUAGE REVIEW UNITS 5 & 6 p.64
Speaking: discussing facts (*world problems*), situational role-play (*organising a charity event*) **Reading**: reading for gist, general comprehension (*magazine article*) **Listening**: true or false (*monologue*) **Writing**: semi-formal letter (*charity*) **Pronunciation**: homophones	Language plus 6 p.96 Exam plus • p.55	
Speaking: picture-based discussion (*technology*), individual long turn (*for and against gadgets*) **Reading**: reading for general understanding, reading for specific information, meaning from context (*magazine article*) **Listening**: identifying arguments for and against (*dialogue*) **Writing**: a 'for and against' essay (*technology*) **Pronunciation**: *r* (silent and pronounced)	Language plus 7 p.98 Exam plus • p.74	LANGUAGE REVIEW UNITS 7 & 8 p.84
Speaking: talking about experiences and opinions (*shopping*), speculating about the future (*how the story ends*) **Reading**: predicting content, general comprehension, matching definitions (*magazine article*) **Listening**: multiple-choice statements (*public speech*) **Writing**: finishing a story (*the New Horizons photostory*) **Pronunciation**: *c* + vowel	Language plus 8 p.100 Exam plus • p.75	

Exam plus resources pp.109–110

The story so far

Objectives

To revise the material covered in Student's Book 3
Summary of the photostory and its characters in the International Young Journalist Competition

Estimated time: 1 hour

The story so far page 4

Warm-up

- If the students have not met each other before, do the following as a warmer for the class.
- Write three sentences about yourself on the board. Two of them should be false and one of them should be true, e.g. *1) I come from London; 2) I like going shopping; 3) I speak three languages.*
- Put the students into groups of three or four and ask them to decide with each other which sentence they think is true. Allow about two minutes for this.
- Ask each group for their answer before telling the class which sentence is true.
- Now ask each student to prepare similar sentences. Go around the class helping with vocabulary as necessary.
- When finished, students work in their groups of three or four to discuss each other's sentences and identify which one is true.

1

- If students have already studied Student's Book 3, write the names of the nine different characters on page 4 on the board. Then, write up the names of the countries they come from in random order.
- Working in pairs, students match each character with their country. When they have finished, ask them to open their books to page 4 to check if they were right.
- If students are new to the story, write *International Young Journalist Competition* on the board. Working in pairs, students briefly discuss what this competition might involve, e.g. young people from different countries, writing articles etc. Get some feedback from the class, putting the main ideas on the board.
- Refer students to page 4 of the book and allow them a few minutes to read about the different characters (you could set them a time limit of three or four minutes). When they have finished, tell them to close their books and ask them some questions about each character to check for understanding:

Ask: Where does Rob come from?
Elicit: He comes from England.
Ask: Where does Rebecca come from?
Elicit: She comes from New Zealand.
Ask: How do they know each other?
Elicit: They're cousins.

- Continue in this way with more questions. If necessary, the students can keep their books open to find the answers more quickly.

Extensions

Group work: favourite characters

Working individually, students rank the characters on page 4 in order of preference. Their favourite character is number 1 and their least favourite character is number 9. Encourage them to think of reasons to explain their choice of favourite and least favourite characters.

When they are ready, students work in small groups of three or four. They compare their rankings, explaining their opinions to each other. Monitor, helping with vocabulary as necessary. Make a note of general errors to address at a later time.

Whole class: introductions

If the students haven't worked together before and don't know each other well, ask them to introduce themselves to each other.

Example:

A Hello. What's your name?
B My name's …

Quick check page 5

Vocabulary

- Students complete exercises 2–3 individually, then check their answers with a partner before you check them in class.

- As exercise 4 tests vocabulary that students may not remember from the previous level, additional help may be needed, so ask students to work in pairs for this exercise. If they still can't figure out the words or phrases, they may ask you for one more letter for each word.

2
1 off   2 in   3 seat   4 attendant   5 landed   6 control
7 officer   8 lounge

3
1 d   2 f   3 a   4 b   5 e   6 c

4
1 solar panel   2 global warming   3 zebra crossing
4 traffic lights   5 memory stick   6 DVD burner
7 terraced house   8 studio flat   9 leisure centre
10 public transport   11 travel insurance
12 lottery ticket   13 work to deadlines
14 customer service   15 forest fire   16 drought

Grammar

- Students complete exercises 5–6 individually, then check their answers with a partner before you check them in class.

- You can use the Quick check page as a diagnostic test to find out if there are any grammar, vocabulary or skills areas covered at previous levels that need further attention.

- If you prefer, you can set any or all the exercises from the Quick check page as homework.

5
1 will   2 might…could   3 don't have to   4 have to
5 rains…will stay   6 arrive…will miss   7 who   8 which
9 will   10 wasn't   11 did   12 long

6
1 were watching…rang   2 called…was surfing
3 has been living   4 have known…were
5 has been raining   6 was doing…started
7 have been published   8 is spoken   9 aren't made
10 written   11 'll have to   12 happens

Topic and vocabulary

Exercise and fitness

Past habits

Skills and ability

Extreme sports

New Zealand

Grammar

used to • past habits

Formation and comparison of adverbs

Verbs with *to*-infinitive or *-ing*

Functions

Talking about past habits

Comparing ability

Talking about lifestyles

Skills and culture/pronunciation

Reading: matching headings, multiple-choice gap-fill

Listening: multiple-choice questions

Speaking: quiz questions

Writing: a paragraph

Pronunciation: *used to*

Estimated time: 7–8 hours

My uncle used to play for the All Blacks pages 6–7

Warm-up

- Students work in pairs. Tell them they have two minutes to think of as many sports as they can where a ball is used, e.g. football, basketball, rugby, tennis, etc. After the two minutes are up, get feedback from each pair, putting their suggestions on the board. Check for understanding and correct pronunciation of each sport.
- Start a brief discussion with the class about the sports, by asking: *Which of the sports do you like best? Which of the sports is most popular in your country?*

1

- Refer students to page 6 and to the title. Ask them where Rebecca comes from and elicit that she comes from New Zealand. Then ask them what they think the All Blacks are and elicit any acceptable responses (see Culture Note below).
- Draw students' attention to the photos and ask them what they think is happening. Elicit that Rebecca and Lisa are going to watch a rugby game.
- Play the recording. Students listen and read the text.

Transcript 1.02

See Student's Book page 6.

CULTURE NOTE **The All Blacks** is the name given to the New Zealand Rugby Union team because the team's uniform is almost all in black. The All Blacks are famous for a traditional Maori dance that they do before each rugby match. This dance is called the **Haka** and it is a version of an old war dance performed before battles.

2 Comprehension check

- Students read the text again and decide if the sentences are true or false, correcting those that are false. They check their answers in pairs. Check answers as a class.
- Ask students why the girls didn't see the match live and elicit that there weren't any tickets left.

KEY

1 F: Rebecca's uncle was an All Blacks rugby player.
2 F: Rebecca went to all her uncle's matches in Auckland.
3 F: Rebecca went to All Blacks matches with her father.
4 T.
5 T.
6 F: The New Zealand team do a dance before the match.

LEARN IT! USE IT! TRANSLATE IT! Ask the students to find the expressions in the text. Check understanding by asking them to give you the equivalent expressions in their language.

Extension

Pair work: dialogue practice

- Play the recording again and ask students to practise the dialogue in closed pairs. Students swap roles when they have finished. Circulate and help with pronunciation and intonation as necessary. Ask a pair of students to act out the dialogue in front of the class.

Grammar Guide • *used to* • past habits

- Check the students' understanding of the structure and use of the affirmative, negative and interrogative forms of *used to*. Point out that in the negative and interrogative forms *used* becomes *use* because of the auxiliary verb *did*.
- Ask students whether *used to* refers to the past, present or future and elicit that it refers to the past. Emphasise that it is normally used to talk about habits which no longer happen, e.g. *I used to go to the beach every summer* means that, in the past, I did it regularly but I no longer do it.

3 Check!

- The students complete the sentences with *use* or *used*. Remind them that we use *used* in the affirmative form only.
- Monitor the students as they work, helping out where necessary. When they have finished, they check their answers in pairs. Check answers as a class.

KEY

1 used 2 use 3 use 4 used 5 use 6 use 7 use
8 used 9 used 10 use

Pronunciation • *used to*

- Unlike the verb *to use*, which is pronounced /juːz/, *used to* is pronounced softly, /ˈjuːstə/. Point out that the *d* is silent as it merges with the *t* in *to*.
1 Students listen to the recording and repeat. Repeat the sentence yourself, focusing on *used to*. Encourage the class to copy your pronunciation.

Transcript 🔊 1.03

See Student's Book page 7.
2 Students listen to the four sentences and repeat. Pause the recording as necessary to allow students time to repeat. Drill the class, choosing different students to repeat each sentence.

Transcript 🔊 1.04

See Student's Book page 7.

4 Vocabulary • exercise and fitness

- Refer students to the table and go through the headings with them, checking for understanding. Point out the list of words and explain that they need to be sorted into the correct column in the table.
- Monitor the students as they work, helping out where necessary. When they have finished, they check their answers in pairs. Check answers as a class.
- Ask students if they can suggest any other words for each column. Allow them 2–3 minutes to brainstorm in pairs and put their suggestions on the board.

KEY

Sports: play volleyball, do gymnastics, go rowing, do aerobics, do yoga
Martial arts: do kick boxing, do Tai Chi, do karate, do judo
Gym activities: do weights, do aerobics, do gymnastics
Adjectives: lazy, sporty, unfit, fit
Places: swimming pool, football pitch, basketball court, rugby pitch, tennis court, squash court, gym

5 What did you use to do?

- Talk to students about your life when you were eight years old and tell them a few things you used to do. You don't have to tell them what you really did, just give them some ideas to help them with the activity, e.g. *When I was eight years old, I used to watch cartoons.*
- Working individually, students think for two minutes about what they used to do when they were eight. Encourage them to make some notes if they want to. Monitor, helping out with ideas or vocabulary as necessary.
- Play the recording. Pause after each question to allow students time to write it down. Play the recording a second time to allow students to check their sentences. Check the answers as a class.
- Working in pairs, students interview each other about when they were eight years old using the questions from the recording. Monitor, listening out for correct use of *used to* in its different forms. Make a note of any common errors to be addressed at the end of the activity.

Transcript 🔊 1.05

See Key.

KEY

1 How did you use to spend your free time?
2 What did you use to watch on TV?
3 Did you use to walk to school?
4 How often did you use to do sport?
5 Which sweets and chocolate did you use to eat?
6 How often did you use to eat fast food?
Students' own answers.

6 Life used to be different

- Refer students to the two photos and ask them what they see. Elicit that there is an elderly man in one photo and a young boy in the other photo. Elicit that the photo of the young boy is very old, and the person in both photos is the same.
- Explain that students have to make notes about the man in the photos under the three headings given. Play the recording. Students compare their notes in pairs.
- Play the recording a second time. Get feedback for each heading from the class.
- Refer students to the question below the photos and allow them time to make notes about their parents' childhood. Monitor, helping out with ideas if they are having difficulty.
- In pairs, students interview each other about their parents' childhood. When they have finished, choose a few stronger students to tell the rest of the class about their partner's parents' childhood.

Transcript 🔊 1.06

Interviewer Was life very different when you were young?
Vic Oh, yes, it was. For example, erm, school was very different then. Classes used to be very big, with at least forty-five children in each class, and teachers used to be very strict. They used to hit us all the time.
Interviewer That's terrible! What about food? Did you use to eat differently in those days?
Vic Well, yes, we did. I suppose the biggest difference was that our mother used to cook twice a day, at lunchtime and in the evening. She used to cook proper food, with fresh ingredients. Everybody buys sandwiches at lunchtime now, and most people eat frozen food at dinnertime, not fresh stuff. And we didn't use to eat any foreign food in those days, because there wasn't any. There weren't any Chinese or Indian restaurants, nothing like that. Now you can eat all kinds of foreign food here.
Interviewer And what about free time?
Vic Well, that was very different. I didn't use to watch TV, because we didn't have one. I used to collect stamps. In fact I've still got an enormous collection. And I used to do a lot of sport. I used to play football in the street with my friends, because there didn't use to be much traffic. Then when I was at secondary school I used to play rugby and go running a lot. I was a lot fitter than my grandchildren are!

KEY

Possible answers:
School:
Classes used to be very big (more than 45 children in each class).
Teachers used to be very strict (hitting children).

Food:
Mother used to cook twice a day, with fresh ingredients.
They didn't use to eat foreign food (no foreign restaurants).
Free time:
They didn't use to watch TV.
He used to collect stamps.
He used to do a lot of sport (football, rugby, running).
Students' own answers.

Extensions

Individual work: research on the past

Tell students to think about a period of history that they would like to have seen. Point out that it doesn't have to be ancient history and that they can choose any period up to, say, the end of the 1980s.

Students do some research on their chosen period. They write a short paragraph describing what people who were living in that period used to do.

If you like, you could encourage students to present their research to the class. Have a vote on the most interesting period chosen.

Group work: he used to take the Tube to school

Tell the class about an imaginary friend of yours. Say that your friend is called Tom and that he was born in London (or an equally busy city that the students will be familiar with). He lived there until he was 22 and then he moved to the countryside because he prefers a quiet lifestyle.

Students work in groups. Ask them to discuss how Tom's life changed. Encourage them to use *used to* as they speak, e.g. Tom used to take the Tube everyday, but now he rides his bicycle everywhere. Encourage them to be creative.

Monitor, helping out with vocabulary or ideas a necessary.

Homework
Workbook pp.4–5 Ex. 1–5
Key p.96

You can swim really well! pages 8–9

Warm-up

- Tell the students about a sport you like doing. For example: *I really like playing tennis. I started it when I was 12 years old and I play every weekend with some friends.*

- Working in pairs, students tell each other about a sport they like doing. Let the activity run for about 2-3 minutes and get some feedback from a few pairs.

7

- Refer students to the photo of Rob and Steve and ask them what they are doing. Elicit that they are swimming in a swimming pool.

- Play the recording. Students listen and read the text.

Transcript 1.07

- See Student's Book page 8.

LEARN IT! USE IT! TRANSLATE IT! Remind the students of these expressions in the dialogue. Check understanding by asking them to give you the equivalent expressions in their language.

8 Comprehension check

- Students read the text again and complete the sentences with the correct name. They check their answers in pairs. Check answers as a class

- Ask the students what Steve thinks he is better at than Rob and elicit that he thinks he is faster at getting changed.

KEY
1 Rob 2 Rob…Steve 3 Steve…Rob 4 Rob…Steve
5 Rob…Steve 6 Rob

Grammar Guide • Formation and comparison of adverbs

- Point out that most adverbs are regular and are formed by adding -ly to the adjective, or that if the adjective ends in -y, they are formed by adding -ily.

- Highlight the irregular forms where the adverb is the same as the adjective. Point out that these forms should be learned. The adverb of *good* is *well*.

- Adverbs usually come after the verb they are describing. When comparing, we add (*much +*) *more* before the adverb, e.g. *I can eat (much) more quickly than you.* If the verb has an object, the adverb follows the object not the verb itself, e.g. *You can play tennis better than me.*

- Draw students' attention to the irregular comparative adverbs and point out that although *badly* is a regular adverb, its comparative form is irregular: *worse*.

9 Check!

- The students put the words into the correct order using the correct adverb form of the adjective in brackets. Check answers as a class.

KEY
2 I play football much better than my brother.
3 Luisa speaks English quite well.
4 My cousin can hit the ball really hard.
5 You play squash worse than me.
6 He can drive much faster than the others.

Extension

Individual work: adjective to adverb

Give any five adjectives to the class, e.g. *beautiful, quiet, noisy, lazy, perfect.* Ask them to write five sentences in which they use the adverb form of the adjectives (if you use the above examples: *beautifully, quietly, noisily, lazily, perfectly*).

Monitor, making sure that students are forming the adverbs correctly and using them logically. Students can compare their sentences in pairs.

---

10 Can you play tennis well?

- Refer students to the photo and ask them who is in it. Elicit that Rob, Steve and a woman are in the photo. Ask them what they think the woman is doing and elicit that she is probably asking the boys some questions.

- Read the instructions with the students and allow them time to go through the chart. Play the recording. Students complete the first two rows of the chart for Rob and Steve. They compare their answers in pairs. Play the recording a second time. Check answers as a class.
- In pairs, students make comparisons between Steve and Rob, using the chart to help them. Monitor, listening out for correct use of comparative adverbs.

Transcript 🔊 1.08

Woman Excuse me. Have you got time to answer a few questions?
Rob Er, yes… What about?
Woman Well, the Council's planning to build a new leisure centre and we're trying to find out about the sports that people do.
Steve OK.
Woman What's your name?
Steve Steve Chang.
Rob And I'm Rob White.
Woman Great! First question: What are your favourite sports, Steve?
Steve I like swimming and tennis.
Woman And are you good at them?
Steve Well, I can swim quite well and I think I play tennis very well.
Woman And what about you, Rob?
Rob I'm the opposite of Steve. I can swim really well. And I can play tennis quite well.
Woman And can either of you play volleyball?
Rob Yes, I can play volleyball but not very well.
Steve No, I've never played volleyball.
Woman And what about martial arts? Do either of you do any martial arts, like judo?
Rob No, we don't.
Steve Well, actually, Rob, I used to do Tai Chi with my grandad when I was younger.
Rob Hey, I didn't know that!
Steve I can't do it very well, though. I haven't done it for ages.
Woman Are there any other sports that you used to do when you were younger? What about you, Rob?
Rob Well, I used to go rowing sometimes with my cousin. But I wasn't very good at it.
Woman And you, Steve?
Steve I used to play football and I still do sometimes. I think I'm quite good at it but I haven't got time to do all the training.
Woman Right, well I think that's enough. Thanks for answering my questions.
Steve That's OK. Bye.
Rob Bye.

KEY
Steve
Not at all: volleyball, judo
Not very well: Tai Chi
Quite well: swimming, football
Very well: tennis
Rob
Not at all: judo
Not very well: rowing, volleyball
Quite well: tennis
Very well: swimming
Students' own answers.

11
- Students work individually to complete the last row in the chart so that it is true for them. Monitor, helping out with vocabulary as necessary.
- When students are ready, they work in pairs and make comparisons about each other's abilities. Monitor, making sure students are forming adverbs and using comparative adverbs correctly.

KEY
Students' own answers.

Extensions

Individual work: adverb to comparative adverb
If you did the previous extension activity, tell students to make five new sentences using the comparative adjective form of the adjectives you gave before.

Monitor, making sure that students are forming the comparative adjectives correctly and using them logically. Students can compare their sentences in pairs.

Group work: cats and dogs
Put the following pairs on the board: cats and dogs, men and women, children and adults. Students work in small groups. Ask them to create three sentences using comparative adjectives for each pair (nine sentences in total). For example, Cats eat more quietly than dogs, or Men drive more dangerously than women.

Monitor, making sure that students are forming the comparative adjectives correctly and using them logically.

When they are ready, ask each group to say their sentences for the rest of the class. Does the rest of the class agree?

ALREADY FINISHED? Students write four sentences to compare their partner's abilities with their own.

Homework
Workbook pp.5–6 Ex.6–10
Key p.96

Talking about lifestyles page 10

12
- Write extreme sports on the board. In pairs, students have 2 minutes to think of as many extreme sports as they can (some possibilities include bungee jumping, skydiving, free-fall parachuting, base jumping, parasailing, free-running, parkour, planking, extreme ironing, etc.)
- Stop the students and get feedback from each pair, putting their suggestions on the board to ensure correct spelling and pronunciation.
- Ask the rest of the class to say if they're familiar with the sports mentioned. If not, the pair who suggested them should explain briefly what they are.
- Ask students where Rebecca comes from and elicit that she comes from New Zealand. Refer them to the article on page 10 and ask them which extreme sport they see in the photo. Elicit that it is a photo of bungee jumping.
- Tell students to skim-read through the text quickly to find out how long Warren has been doing bungee jumping. Remind them to aim for a general understanding and not

to worry about unknown words. After no more than 1 minute stop the students and elicit that Warren has been doing bungee jumps since he was at school.

13 Comprehension check

- Allow students time to read the sentences. Encourage them to identify key words that will help them locate their answers in the text. They decide if the sentences are true or false and compare their answers in pairs. Check answers as a class.
- Ask the students to briefly discuss what they think of Warren and to choose any three adjectives to describe him.

KEY

1 T.
2 F: He doesn't go free-fall parachuting often because it's too expensive.
3 T.
4 T.
5 F: Rebecca doesn't want to try bungee jumping.

Extension

Pair work: vocabulary building

Tell the students to find the following adjectives in the text in exercise 12: *conservative, eccentric, incredible, compulsive*. Ask them to try to guess the meaning of the words from their context and to check their ideas in pairs. Allow them to check the meanings in a dictionary.

Working individually, they try to think of one person they know that can be described by each adjective. When they are ready, they tell their partners about the people they have chosen. Encourage them to explain why they chose these people for these adjectives.

Monitor, helping out as necessary and making a note of any general errors you wish to address later.

LANGUAGE TIP Point out that verbs can either be used in the *to-* infinitive (*to do*) or in the *-ing* form (*doing*) when they follow other verbs. This depends on the verb that they follow. These verbs must be learned.

---

14 *to*-infinitive or *–ing*?

- Students read the sentence halves and match them together. Encourage them to look for a logical link if they are not sure whether they are supposed to take the *to-* infinitive or the *-ing* form.
- They check their answers in pairs. Check answers as a class.

KEY

1 b 2 f 3 e 4 a 5 c 6 d 7 g 8 h

15 I like having free time

- Tell students that they are going to listen to a girl called Natasha talk about her free time. Allow them time to read the incomplete sentences.
- When they are ready, play the recording. Students complete the sentences with the verbs that Natasha uses. They check their answers in pairs. Play the recording a second time. Check answers as a class.

- Students write six sentences of their own using the first verb in the sentences from the listening exercise. Monitor, helping out as necessary and checking for correct use of verb forms.
- When students are ready, they work in pairs to guess each other's sentences.

Transcript 🔊 1.09

Natasha Well, the first thing that I have to say is that I hate doing sport. I really detest it. I quite like being lazy! I really love getting up late on Saturday mornings. Then I do absolutely nothing. Well, I suppose that's not true, because I have breakfast and I quite like chatting to my friends on my mobile. I also listen to music. I really like listening to music. I refuse to go to the gym with my friends. I can't stand all the horrible noises people make! A few months ago I started going to school by bike because I couldn't afford to get the bus – I spent all my money on CDs! But I stopped cycling to school in November. It's far too cold in the winter! I want to take driving lessons soon and I hope to buy a car next summer. But that means I have to get a job to earn some money and well, you know, I really like having lots of free time…

KEY

1 hate doing
2 like being
3 love getting up
4 like listening
5 refuse to go
6 started going
7 afford to get
8 stopped cycling
9 want to take
10 hope to buy
Students' own answers.

ALREADY FINISHED? Students organise the verbs under the correct headings. Encourage them to check their answers in a dictionary and point out that, if they are not sure, using a dictionary is a useful way of finding out what structure different verbs take.

KEY

-ing: admit, finish, suggest, avoid, mind
to-infinitive: pretend, arrange, seem, decide, learn

Extensions

Individual work: I'm pretending to study…

Tell students to make a sentence using each of the verbs in the *Already finished?* box. Remind them to use the correct form of the verb that follows them.

Monitor, helping out as necessary and making a note of any general errors you wish to address later.

Whole class: Stand up, sit down

Allow students two or three minutes to look over the verbs they have covered in exercises 14, 15 and in the *Already finished?* box on page 10.

Ask students to close their books and divide the class into two groups. One group is the *to*-infinitive group and the other group is the *-ing* group.

Call out different verbs from the lesson at random. If the verb you call out is followed by the *to*-infinitive form, then that group must immediately stand up. The same goes for the other group. Any student who stands up at the wrong time is eliminated. Continue the activity for about 10 verbs. The winning team is the team with the most students left.

Homework
Workbook pp.6–7 Ex.11–13
Key pp.96–97

Grammar Check (page 11)

used to

1
affirmative: subject + *used to* + base form
negative: subject + *didn't use to* + base form
interrogative: *Did* + subject + *use to* + base form

2
1 He used to work
2 I didn't use to do
3 Did she use to go
4 I used to spend
5 They didn't use to eat
6 Did he use to play

Adverbs

3
1 verbs
2 *-ly*
3 We change *–y* to *–ily*.
4 fast, hard
5 fast, hard, well

4
1 They won the match easily.
2 I wrote his address carefully.
3 Allan banged his head hard.
4 She did the exercise quickly.
5 The train from Bath to London goes fast.
6 Tanya can play the violin well.

5
1 I can play volleyball better than you.
2 He can swim faster than me.
3 I speak French more fluently than you.
4 Chloë sings more beautifully than Jessica.
5 ✓
6 My sister works harder than me.

Verbs + *to*-infinitive or *-ing*

6
to-infinitive: refuse, want, afford, hope, promise, try
-ing: hate, love, stop, keep, like, start

7
1 eating   2 to take   3 learning   4 doing   5 to move
6 to buy

Homework
Workbook p.7 Revision
Key p.97

Skills and culture (pages 12–13)

Warm-up

- If you have time, find a simple map of New Zealand on the Internet (preferably without nearby countries, and remember to blank out the name of the country if it is written on the map) and print it out. Show it to the students and ask them what country it is. Elicit that it is New Zealand. Ask them where it is and elicit that it is in the Southern Hemisphere, beside Australia.

- In pairs, allow students one or two minutes to discuss what they know about New Zealand. Get some feedback from each pair.

1 Reading

- Students open their books on page 12. Refer them to the quiz and ask them to complete it. They compare their answers in pairs. Tell students to turn to page 111 to check their answers to the quiz questions.

- Ask students if they are surprised by any of the answers.

KEY
1 b   2 a   3 a   4 b   5 a

> **CULTURE NOTE** **New Zealand** is an English speaking country. It was colonised by the British in the 19th century and it is a member of the Commonwealth. This means that the British monarch is also the head of state of New Zealand.

2

- Draw students' attention to the four paragraphs A–D and to the four questions. Explain that they should skim-read the paragraphs and match the questions to the paragraphs. Allow no more than one or two minutes for this.

- Students check their answers in pairs. Check answers as a class.

KEY
A Where are the Maoris from?
B What's the Maori language like?
C What is the Haka?

D What is Ta Moko?

3

• Read the Study Strategy with the class. Students read the text again and complete the gaps with the correct word.

• Students check their answers in pairs. Then check answers as a class.

KEY

1 d **2** c **3** b **4** c **5** a **6** d **7** a **8** b

4

• Draw students' attention to the highlighted words in the text. Remind them that instead of using a dictionary, it is quicker and more effective to use the context of an unknown word to work out its meaning.

• Students match the words to their synonyms or definitions. They check their answers in pairs. Check answers as a class.

KEY

1 menacingly **2** warriors **3** status **4** scare **5** motifs **6** canoes **7** proudly **8** belief

5 Listening

• Tell students they are going to listen to a radio show about films related to New Zealand. Allow them time to read the first multiple-choice question. When they are ready, play the recording until the // symbol. Ask students what the correct answer is and elicit that the correct answer is c.

• Allow students time to read the rest of the questions, pointing out that they should identify key words to help them as they listen. When they are ready, play the recording from the beginning. They check their answers in pairs.

• Play the recording a second time. Check the answers with the whole class.

Transcript 🎧 1.10

Radio DJ Good evening and welcome to Fanatical for Film. This week we have Amelia Russell in the studio to talk to us about films and actors from New Zealand. Amelia's a film critic from Auckland, and she's just written a book about the New Zealand film industry. Amelia, welcome to Fanatical for Film.

Amelia Thanks. It's a pleasure to be here.

Radio DJ So Amelia, we usually think of Hollywood as the centre of the film world, but recently New Zealand has had its share of success.

Amelia Yes, it has. If someone says the word 'blockbuster', most people probably think of Hollywood films like *Star Wars* and *Mission Impossible* first of all, but three of the biggest and most successful films of recent years are the *Lord of the Rings* trilogy, which were all made in New Zealand. //

Radio DJ How about stars? Again, a lot of people think all famous film stars are American.

Amelia Well, it's true that probably the majority of film stars are American, but there are a lot of stars from other countries too. Cate Blanchett and Nicole Kidman are very famous Australians, for example. The biggest name from New Zealand is probably Russell Crowe, who starred in *Gladiator* and won an Oscar for his role in *A Beautiful Mind*.

Radio DJ Directors from New Zealand seem to be having the most success, though.

Amelia Yes. The first breakthrough was by Jane Campion, who won an Oscar for *The Piano* and then went on to direct Nicole Kidman in *The Portrait of a Lady*, from the novel by Henry James. There's also Andrew Adamson, who directed *Shrek* 1 and 2, and the first Narnia film, *The Lion, the Witch and the Wardrobe*. Then there's *Casino Royale*. That's a very international film, with the British actor Daniel Craig as James Bond, and a French star, Eva Green, as the woman he falls in love with. It's been a huge success – it took more money on its first weekend than any other James Bond film ever – so that's a great achievement by its director, Martin Campbell, who's also from New Zealand. And it seems that Peter Jackson, who directed *The Lord of the Rings* films and *King Kong* and is also from New Zealand, may end up being as successful as American directors like Steven Spielberg and George Lucas. He, above all, is really putting New Zealand on the map!

Radio DJ Finally, are there any films about New Zealand that you'd like to recommend to our listeners?

Amelia Yes, my personal favourite is *Once Were Warriors*. It's a film about how difficult life is for Maoris in New Zealand today and although it isn't as famous as *The Piano* or the *Lord of the Rings* films, in my opinion it's the best film ever made in New Zealand.

KEY

1 c **2** c **3** b **4** b **5** c **6** a **7** a

6 Speaking

• Tell students to work in pairs and to think of films from their country. Allow them a few minutes to talk about famous films, actors or directors that they know.

• After a few minutes, tell each pair to prepare six questions about films and actors from their country. Monitor, helping out with ideas or vocabulary where necessary. Check that students are forming their questions correctly.

• When they are ready, they join another pair and exchange questions. Each pair has to answer the other pair's quiz.

• Get feedback from a few pairs.

7 Writing

• Students choose an actor from their own country that they admire. They write a short paragraph about their favourite actor. You might like to encourage them to do some Internet research on their chosen actor and set the activity for homework.

| Extension
| Language plus p.86

Exam plus 1

Objectives

To practise exams related to the material covered in Unit 1

Reading: Missing sentences

Listening: True or false

Speaking: Picture-based discussion

Reading • Missing sentences page 14

Warm-up

- Write the word *fitness* on the board and ask the students what type of word it is. Elicit that it is a noun. Ask them what the adjective form is and elicit that it is *fit*.
- Working in pairs, students have one minute to think of different ways of keeping fit. Get some feedback from each pair, putting their suggestions on the board.

1

- Draw students' attention to the title of the text and ask them what they think the text will be about. Elicit that it will probably be about an achievement that somebody has made and that they feel good about it. Remind students that they should use any titles or pictures to help them get an overall understanding of a text.
- Write this question on the board: *Why did Darren use to feel left out at school?* Tell the students to skim-read the text quickly to find the answer. Explain that when they skim-read, they should try to get the main idea from the text by reading quickly and selectively. Set them a time limit of about one or two minutes, depending on the strength of the class. Elicit that Darren felt left out because he was overweight and couldn't take part in sports.
- Read the instructions for the task with the students and draw their attention to sentences A–F. Make sure students understand the task fully.
- Tell the students that as they now have a general idea of the text from their skim-read, they can start to do the task. Allow them time to read through the sentences and ask them to underline key words that will help them insert the sentences into the correct gaps.
- When students are ready, do the first gap together as an example. Ask students to read the sentences around the first gap and to choose the best one from the options. Elicit that C is the correct answer because Darren talks about primary school. He then goes on to compare it to High School, so C must be the correct answer.
- Students continue with the remaining gaps and complete them. Remind them that there is one extra sentence they do not need. They check their answers in pairs. Check answers as a class.

KEY

1 C   **2** E   **3** D   **4** A   **5** F

> **EXAM TIP** It's always important for the students to get an overall understanding of a text before they begin to do the task. They should look for grammatical links (such as comparative adverbs or adjectives) and logical links between the missing sentences and the text surrounding the gap.

Listening • True or false page 14

Warm-up

- Tell the students to imagine that they are going to join a new gym. In pairs, they have two minutes to brainstorm the different things they would like the gym to have, e.g. swimming pool, weights, exercise bikes, etc.
- Get some feedback from a few pairs. Can anybody think of any disadvantages of being a member of a gym?

2

- Tell students that they are going to listen to a conversation between Mike and Sara about joining a gym. Read the instructions carefully with the class and make sure they understand what is required.
- Draw their attention to the statements 1–8 and allow them time to read through them carefully. Remind them to underline keywords to help them focus on the listening and to identify relevant sections where they can find their answers.
- Explain that the words they hear on the recording may not be the same as the words in the statements. Encourage them to be aware of synonyms for the keywords they have identified in the statements.
- Do the first statement as an example for the class. Play the recording until the // symbol. Allow students a little time to decide on their answer. Play the same segment a second time for students to check. Elicit that the correct answer is *True* as Mike says he is filling out an application to join a health and fitness centre.
- Remind students that they will hear the recording twice so that if they are not sure about an answer during the first listening, they shouldn't worry as they will hear it a second time.
- Play the recording from the beginning. Students do the task and check their answers in pairs. Play the recording a second time. Check answers as a class. If the class is weaker, you may like to play the recording a third time as you check the answers for students to see why the answer is true or false.

Transcript 🔊 1.11

Mike Hey Sara. How are you?

Sara Oh, hi Mike. I'm great, thanks. How about you? What are you doing?

Mike I'm okay, thanks. I'm just filling out an application form for the health and fitness centre in the town centre. //

Sara Oh, really? But I heard that it's very expensive! My sister Jessica joined two months ago and she's paying more than £60 a month. And not only that, she also had to pay the membership fee of £120! I wouldn't pay that much money!

Mike Well, I think the price depends on what activities you do. Maybe Jessica is taking aerobics classes and has access to the swimming pool. All I want is a basic membership – somewhere to do weights! So it'll probably be cheaper for me.

Sara Maybe. But I still think it's a waste of money. There are so many other ways to exercise. Just go for a jog in the mornings, or ride your bike. I think that kind of working out is much healthier. And what's more, it's free!

Mike Yes, it's free. That's true. But it's also difficult. Do you go jogging or cycling in the rain?

Sara Well, no, but that's not the point. I just think you could save your money for something else. Like a holiday or something.

Mike Oh, I don't think it's a bad idea to pay for keeping fit. It's very important to keep your body active and healthy you know. And anyway, these days I spend so much of my time studying and concentrating on revision that I rarely get any exercise at all. I think that if I join it will force me to keep more active.

Sara I suppose you've got a point. Well, good luck with it. Oh, I almost forgot to tell you, some of us are thinking about going to a concert in London the weekend after the exams. I forget the name of the band, but it would be fun to celebrate the end of term. Fancy joining us?

Mike Oh, that sounds fun. Do you know how much the tickets are?

Sara I think they're £40, with a £5 discount for students. So, we'll be able to pay less.

Mike Hmmm. I'd really love to go! But I'll have to think about it. I might not be able to afford it now I'm joining the gym.

Sara See! Told you it was too expensive!

KEY

1 T   2 F   3 F   4 T   5 F   6 F   7 T   8 T

> **EXAM TIP** It's important to read the question and statements carefully before you listen. Identifying key words helps students to focus on the recording and to follow it. Remind them that they will normally hear the recording twice, so that they can listen more carefully in the second listening if they didn't get the answer the first time.

Speaking • Picture-based discussion page 109

Warm-up

- Students work in pairs. Ask them to tell each other about how they normally keep fit and what exercise they do.
- After one or two minutes, get feedback from a few pairs by asking a few students to describe how their partner keeps fit.

3

- Tell students to turn to page 109 and draw their attention to the three pictures on the left. Ask them what they can see and elicit a brief description of each photo from the class.
- Read the instructions with the class and read through the prompts with them. Make sure they understand what they have to do.
- Remind them that they are going to use the photos along with the prompts to discuss how people can keep fit. They should remember that while the prompts are in question form, they should not simply be answered directly but should help to generate ideas that can support the discussion. Point out that they should try to speak about each of the ideas mentioned in the prompts.
- Divide students into small groups of three or four and tell them to start the task. Monitor the students as they discuss. Make a note of any general errors students make, and observe how they link their ideas together. Try not to interrupt the students too much in their discussion.

- When students have finished, get some feedback from each group about the main ideas they discussed. If you like, and if the students are able, you could bring the discussion to a class level for a few minutes to round off the activity.

> **EXAM TIP** Emphasise that this activity is not about describing the pictures but that it is about discussing the ideas in the guiding questions. The pictures are there to help generate ideas along with the prompts and are just the basis for the discussion.

Functions bank
Workbook p.51

Further exam practice
Workbook pp.12–13

Exam plus 2

Objectives
To practise exams related to the material covered in Unit 2
Use of English: Open cloze
Writing: Review
Speaking: Picture description and picture comparison

Use of English • Open cloze page 15

Warm-up

- Write *phobia* on the board and ask the students if they know what it means. Explain that a phobia is something we are afraid of without having a good reason for it. In pairs, students think of common phobias that people may have (it isn't necessary for them to give the technical term, i.e. *spiders* is just as good as *arachnophobia* at this stage).
- Get feedback from each pair. Does anybody in the class have a phobia of anything?

1

- Draw students' attention to the text. Remind them that it is always important to skim-read any text before they read it in detail, as this will help them understand the text as a whole. Tell students to read the text quickly, ignoring the gaps. Ask them whether people with a phobia can be treated or not. Elicit that phobias can be treated.
- Read the instructions with the students and make sure they understand that they need only one word for each gap. Point out that in this type of task, the missing words are generally words like prepositions, pronouns, quantifiers and common verbs. In other words, they will already know the word that is missing.
- Look at the first gap together with the students as an example and read the first sentence carefully. Ask them what kind of word they think they will need in the gap. Elicit that they will probably need a preposition. Ask them if they know which proposition follows *afraid*. If they don't, tell them to use *afraid* in a different sentence, e.g. *I am afraid … spiders*, and explain that this may help them. Elicit that the missing word is *of*.

- Students complete the rest of the gaps and check their answers in pairs. Check answers as a class, making sure that students understand why each word is correct.

KEY
1 of   **2** the   **3** are   **4** with   **5** to   **6** have   **7** a   **8** is
9 are   **10** is

> **EXAM TIP** Students should always begin by reading the whole text quickly. A general understanding is necessary to see how the text fits together and therefore is necessary to identify the correct answer.

Writing • Review page 15

Warm-up

- Ask the students to work in pairs and discuss whether they like scary films or not. Encourage them to say why they like or don't like them.
- Get some feedback from each pair about scary films. Ask: *What's the scariest film you have ever seen?*

2

- Read the instructions with the students and go through the prompts with them. Make sure they understand the information they have to include.
- Point out that a review has a simple structure. They should introduce the film or book at the beginning and then go on to summarise what it's about. They should then say why they think this film or book is scary and then finish by recommending it or not.
- Encourage students to make a quick plan for their review. This is important so that they don't forget any important or interesting information. The plan will help them keep focused on the task.
- When students are ready, they write their reviews. Allow them about 15–20 minutes to write it, depending on the strength of the students. Alternatively, students can do it for homework and bring the review to the next class for correction.
- Remind them that they should always leave some time at the end of a writing activity to read what they've written to check for mistakes.

Speaking • Picture description and picture comparison page 15

Warm-up

- Students work in pairs. Ask them to think about a scary or stressful situation that they have experienced at some time. Allow them 2–3 minutes to compare ideas.
- When students have finished, get feedback from each pair. Ask: *Which situation do you think was most stressful?*

3

- Draw students' attention to the two photos on page 15. Ask them what they see and elicit that one photo is of students taking an exam, while the other photo is of a girl at the dentist's.
- Read the instructions with the students and make sure they understand the task. Point out the four prompts

and explain they need to use these as they describe their pictures.

- At this stage, it might be a good idea to remind students of phrases they can use to describe and speculate about a picture. Elicit suitable phrases from the students and put them on the board, e.g. *In the foreground/background …, It looks like …, It seems like …,* etc.
- Divide students into A/B pairs. Allow them some time to look at their photos and to think about what they are going to say. When they are ready, students A describe their photo to students B. They then swap so students B describe their photo to students A.
- Monitor the students as they describe their pictures. Make sure they refer to all of the pieces of information in their description. Make a note of any general errors you may want to come back to later.
- Choose one or two stronger students to describe each picture for the rest of the class.

4

- Read the task with the students and go through the prompts with them. Make sure they understand that they have to compare and contrast both pictures, not just describe them. This means they will have to look for similar and different features between the two pictures.
- Point out that they should link the prompts to the pictures to help them in their comparison. For example, they can make a speculation about why exams are stressful and refer to the picture to exemplify this.
- Remind students that they will need to use comparative language in their comparison and phrases to make contrasts, e.g. *In picture A… However, in picture B…, While the people in picture A are …, the people in picture B are …,* etc.
- Students remain in their A/B pairs. Students A compare and contrast the two pictures first while students B listen. They then swap.
- Monitor the students as they make their comparisons. Try not to interrupt, but be ready to help any struggling students with ideas to keep them speaking. When students have finished, choose a few stronger students to perform the task for the rest of the class.

> **EXAM TIP** Make sure students realise that they do not need to accurately describe the picture in detail. If they are unsure about something, they can speculate. They are being tested on their speaking ability, not on their knowledge of the content of the picture. For this reason, it's good to have prepared useful phrases for speculating.

Further exam practice
Workbook p.12–13

UNIT 2

Topic and vocabulary

The body

Appearance

Advice

Health, illness, remedies

Body image

Grammar

have/get something *done*

should/ought to

Functions

Getting things done

Giving advice

Talking about health

Skills and culture/pronunciation

Speaking: conversation

Reading: predicting content, comprehension questions

Listening: true or false

Writing: email

Pronunciation: vowel sounds

Estimated time: 7–8 hours

Have you had your hair dyed?

pages 16–17

Warm-up

- Students work in pairs. Ask them to discuss their appearance and to choose one thing about it that they would like to change.
- Get some feedback from a few pairs, putting any new vocabulary on the board.

1

- Refer students to page 16 and to the photo of Rob and Amar. Ask them what they think Rob is doing and elicit that he is looking at his hair in the shop window.
- Play the recording. Students listen and read the text.

Transcript 🔊 1.12

See Student's Book page 16.

LEARN IT! USE IT! TRANSLATE IT! Ask the students to find the expressions in the text. Check understanding by asking them to give you the equivalent expressions in their language.

2 Comprehension check

- Students read the text again and decide if the sentences are true or false, correcting those that are false. They check their answers in pairs. Check answers as a class.
- Ask students what Rob thinks would be a problem if he had his nose pierced and elicit that he thinks it would be difficult to blow his nose.

KEY

1 T.

2 T.

3 F: He would like to have a tattoo done.

4 F: In India brides usually have henna tattoos done.

5 F: He would like to have his nose pierced.

6 F: He's going to have it taken in the shop.

> **CULTURE NOTE** **Henna tattoos** are a common form of body art in India. They are not permanent tattoos, as the dye stays on the surface of the skin instead of being inserted underneath the skin, like regular tattoos.

3 Vocabulary • the body

- Refer students to the picture of Rob and to the different parts of the body in the box. They match the words to the correct parts of the body.
- When they have finished, they check their answers in pairs. Play the recording to check answers as a class.

Transcript 🔊 1.13

See Student's Book page 16 and key.

KEY

1 hair 2 eye 3 ear 4 tooth/teeth 5 lip 6 neck

7 chin 8 shoulder 9 arm 10 elbow 11 stomach

12 bottom 13 leg 14 foot/feet 15 toe 16 wrist

17 hand 18 finger 19 thumb 20 nail 21 chest

22 mouth 23 nose 24 eyebrow

> ## Extension
>
> ### Whole class: Simple Simon
>
> Play Simple Simon with the class. Tell the students to close their books and ask them all to stand up.
>
> Explain that you are going to say an instruction from Simple Simon and that the students have to do what he says. For example, *Simple Simon says put your hand on your neck.* The students have to put their hands on their necks. The game continues in this manner, using different parts of the body each time. After the first three or four sentences, make it harder by saying the sentences more quickly.
>
> If any student gets the wrong part of the body, they are eliminated.
>
> You may want to remind students that if you don't start your instructions with the words *Simple Simon says…*, they don't have to perform the action.

Grammar Guide • have/get something done

- Check the students' understanding of the structure and use of the affirmative, negative and interrogative forms of *have/get* something *done* in the different tenses. Point out that *done* is the past participle form of the verb, not the past simple.
- Tell students to refer to the text in exercise 1 again and ask them who is going to take Rob's photo. Elicit that somebody in the shop is going to take Rob's photo: *I need to have my photo taken.* This means that somebody else is going to do it for Rob, and that he is going to pay for it. We normally use this structure to say we are paying for some sort of service.

4 Check!

- Students complete the sentences using the correct form of the verbs in brackets. They check their answers in pairs. Check answers as a class.

KEY

1 had/got…taken 2 haven't had/haven't got…pierced
3 had/got…dyed 4 have/get…done
5 'm having/'m getting…painted 6 has/gets…tested

Extension

Pair work: I'd have a new house built

Students work in pairs. Tell them to imagine that they have won €1 million in a competition. In their pairs, they think of five things that they would have done with the money.

Monitor, helping out with vocabulary and ideas as necessary.

---

5 I haven't had it done yet

- Refer students to the list of nouns and verbs. Explain that each noun will match to one of the verbs. Ask the class what verb logically matches with *hair* and elicit that the verb is *cut*.
- Working individually, students match the rest of the nouns and verbs. Monitor, helping out as necessary. When they have finished, they check their answers in pairs. Check answers as a class.
- Ask the students what kind of situation they think would be suitable for using these noun/verb combinations. Elicit any acceptable responses at this stage.

KEY

1 d 2 f 3 g 4 e 5 a 6 b 7 j 8 i 9 h 10 c

6

- Divide students into A/B pairs. Read the instructions with the class and refer students A to page 111 and students B to page 108. Make sure each student knows their role and what they are supposed to do.
- Remind students of the verb/noun combinations in the previous exercise and explain that they are preparing for a music gig. In their pairs, they use their respective information to ask and answer each other about their preparations for the gig. Remind them to use *have/get* something *done* and the words from exercise 5.

- Monitor the students as they speak, listening out for correct use of the structure. Make a note of any general errors to address at the end of the activity.

KEY
Students' own answers.

7 She's had lots of things done

- Draw students' attention to the two pictures and tell them to imagine that this is their singer. Ask the students which picture looks more like that of a singer in a pop group and elicit that the picture on the right looks more suitable.
- In pairs, students quickly identify differences between the two pictures. After one or two minutes, get feedback from each pair about what's different.
- Students complete the dialogue using the correct form of the verbs in the box. They check their answers in pairs. Play the recording to check answers as a class.

Transcript 🔊 1.14

See Student's Book page 17 and key.

KEY

1 's had…cut 2 's had…dyed 3 's had…done
4 's had…pierced 5 's had…done 6 get…removed

Extension

Pair work: dialogue practice

Play the recording again and ask students to practise the dialogue in closed pairs. Students swap roles when they have finished. Circulate and help with pronunciation and intonation as necessary. Ask a pair of students to act out the dialogue in front of the class.

ALREADY FINISHED? Students think about their own lives and make a list of the things they've had done over the past month. When they've finished, they compare their lists with their partners.

Homework
Workbook pp.8–9 Ex.1–5
Key p.97

You should let go! pages 18–19

Warm-up

- Tell the students about a small problem that you have. It doesn't have to be a real problem, just something to make them think. For example, *I've got a problem. I'm going to a good friend's party next weekend and I'm really looking forward to it, but I've just found out that my aunt wants to see me. She's come all the way from Canada. I don't know what to do!*
- Working in pairs, students think about a piece of advice to give you. After one minute, get a piece of advice from each student. Have a vote on the best piece of advice.

8

- Refer students to the photo of Emily and Lisa and ask them what they are doing. Elicit that they are having coffee together. Ask them what they think they are talking about. Elicit any acceptable responses (they seem to be talking about something serious).

- Play the recording. Students listen and read the text.

Transcript 🔘 1.15

See Student's Book page 18.

LEARN IT! USE IT! TRANSLATE IT! Remind the students of these expressions in the dialogue. Check understanding by asking them to give you the equivalent expressions in their language.

9 Comprehension check

- Students read the text again and answer the questions. They check their answers in pairs. Check answers as a class.
- Ask the students how they think Emily feels when Lisa says that Rob likes her. Elicit that she probably feels shocked or surprised or possibly angry.

KEY

1 Yes, she does.
2 Because Emily treated him pretty badly.
3 No, she doesn't.
4 She thinks Emily should forget about him, move on and start looking for somebody else.
5 She thinks Rob likes her.

Grammar Guide • *should, ought to*

- Explain that when we give advice, we can use *should* and *ought to*. In this context, they have exactly the same meaning, although *ought to* is normally only used in affirmative sentences. Check that students understand the affirmative, interrogative and negative structures of *should* and *ought to*. Point out that we do not use the infinitive with *to* after *should*.
- Draw students' attention to the other phrases for giving advice and make sure they understand their structure. Explain that they are useful as it is good to use different phrases instead of just using *should* or *ought to* all the time

10 Check!

- Students rewrite the sentences using the words in brackets. They check answers in pairs. Check answers as a class.

KEY

1 You should sit down for a while.
2 You ought to buy her some flowers.
3 If I were you, I'd split up with him.
4 You'd better go to bed.
5 You shouldn't sunbathe without protection.
6 Why don't you eat your breakfast first?

11 If I were you...

- Refer students to the incomplete dialogue and explain that Caroline is giving Alice some advice. Ask them to read the dialogue quickly to find out what Alice wants to do. Elicit that she wants to get fit.
- Students complete the dialogue with suitable words. They check their answers in pairs. Play the recording to check answers as a class.

- In pairs, students practise the dialogue. Monitor, helping out with pronunciation as necessary. When students have finished, choose a stronger pair or two to act out the dialogue for the class.

Transcript 🔘 1.16

See Student's Book page 19 and Key.

KEY

1 should...do 2 ought to go 3 don't you go
4 were you, I'd go 5 better stop

LOOK OUT! This is a common mistake for students at this level. Emphasise that we cannot say ~~an advice~~ or ~~advices~~. Instead we use *some advice* or, if we want to make it countable, we can say *a piece of advice*. Similar uncountable nouns that can be confused are *information*, *work*, *equipment* and *research*.

Extension

Individual work: uncountable nouns

Tell students to make two sentences for each of the uncountable nouns mentioned above in connection with the *Look out!* box (*advice, information, work, equipment, research*). Write the nouns on the board for reference. Monitor, helping out with vocabulary and ideas as necessary.

12 What should I do?

- Divide students into groups of four. If the groups don't divide evenly, you can have one or two groups of three.
- Each student in a group chooses a different problem. The other students in the group give advice for that problem. Allow students some time to think and make notes if necessary. Monitor, helping with ideas or vocabulary where needed.
- When students are ready, they begin the activity. Encourage them to use a variety of structures for giving their advice and make sure they are using them correctly. Each group decides on the best piece of advice for each problem. Monitor, helping where necessary and making a note of any general errors to be addressed at the end of the activity.
- Get some feedback from each group about the advice they though was best. Which group in the class had the most creative/helpful advice?

KEY

Students' own answers.

ALREADY FINISHED? Students write a paragraph giving advice to someone with one of the problems in exercise 12. Encourage them to use different phrases so that it sounds more natural.

Extension

Pair work: If I were Emily, I'd…

In pairs, students imagine that they are having a coffee with Emily and Lisa in exercise 8 on page 18. They think of advice that they would give to Emily. Encourage them to think of different ideas than those that Lisa suggested.

Monitor, helping out with vocabulary and ideas as necessary.

| Homework
Workbook pp.9–10 Ex.6–10
Key p.98

Talking about health page 20

13 Vocabulary • illnesses

- Draw students' attention to the picture of the classroom at the top of the page and ask them what they notice about it. Elicit that there are only two students in the class. Ask them why they think it is so empty and elicit that the other students may be ill.
- In pairs, students discuss the last time they missed school because of illness. After one or two minutes, get some feedback from a few pairs.
- Refer students to the pictures of the students who are ill. In pairs, they match a health problem to each person. Play the recording for students to check their answers.
- In their pairs, students ask and answer questions about each ill student. Monitor, helping out with pronunciation where necessary. Make sure students are using the right verbs with the right illnesses.

Transcript 1.17

Teacher Jenny?
Liam Jenny's absent, Miss. She's got stomach ache.
Teacher OK. Paul?
Paul Here, Miss.
Teacher Joe?
Liam He's got a cold.
Teacher Susan? Trinny?
Liam They're both with the school nurse. Susan feels sick. Trinny's got a headache.
Teacher Simon?
Paul He's got a temperature.
Teacher Are you kidding?
Paul No, he phoned me last night.
Teacher Liam?
Liam Here, Miss.
Teacher Good! Fred?
Paul He's absent. He's got a sore throat and a cough.
Teacher Tony?
Liam He's broken his leg.
Teacher Elizabeth?
Liam She's got terrible backache and Claire's shoulder hurts. They had an accident playing basketball.
Teacher I can't believe it! Robert?
Paul He's absent too. He's got toothache.
Teacher What's the matter with you all? Mmm, let me check the register… Oh, I see! You've got a Maths test this morning!

KEY
1 Fred 2 Simon 3 Jenny 4 Joe 5 Trinny
6 Robert 7 Susan 8 Elizabeth 9 Claire 10 Tony

Extension

Whole class: illnesses

Have a brainstorming session with the class. Divide them into two teams. Each team should choose one of their members to go to the board.

Tell the teams that they have to tell their students at the board as many other illnesses that they can think of in two minutes. The students at the board have to write what their teams tell them. Tell them not to worry about spelling at this stage. When the two minutes are up, stop the brainstorm. The team with the most illnesses on the board wins.

Go through the words on the board with the class, making any corrections to spelling as necessary.

14 Vocabulary • remedies

- Refer students to the list of phrases and ask them what they think the word *remedy* means. Elicit that a remedy is something that will hopefully cure us if we are ill.
- Allow students some time to read through the remedies and check for understanding. In pairs, students match the illnesses in exercise 13 to a suitable remedy.
- Get some feedback from the class for each illness. Do they agree with each other's suggested remedies?

KEY
Students' own answers.

15 I'm not feeling very well

- Draw students' attention to the jumbled dialogue. Explain that they need to put it into the correct order. Students check their dialogues in pairs. Play the recording to check the correct order as a class.
- Working in pairs, students use the dialogue structure to practise talking about the different illnesses and remedies from exercises 13 and 14. Encourage them to practise using different phrases for giving advice.
- Monitor, helping out as necessary and making a note of any errors to be addressed at the end of the activity. When students have finished, choose one or two students to act out their dialogues for the class. Have a vote on the best/ funniest dialogue.

Transcript 1.18

See Student's Book page 20 and Key.

KEY
1 Are you OK?
2 No, I'm not feeling very well.
3 What's the matter?
4 I've got a headache.
5 Why don't you take some painkillers and go to bed?
6 Yes, I think I will.

Extension

Whole class: doctors and patients

Divide the class into two groups. One group consists of doctors and the other group consists of patients. Tell the patients to choose an illness (they shouldn't change it once they've chosen one). Tell the doctors to choose a remedy (they can only have one remedy) without knowing what illness they'll have to cure.

Explain that the patients need to find a doctor who can cure them. Tell the students to mingle: the patients need to explain what's wrong and the doctors need to give advice. When a patient finds a suitable doctor they sit down.

Monitor, listening out for correct use of language and helping where necessary.

Pronunciation • vowel sounds

1 Draw students' attention to the three words in the chart. Point out that although each word contains the letter *o*, they are pronounced differently and that it is important to be able to pronounce vowel sounds correctly. Play the recording. Pause after each of the words and repeat the word yourself. Try to move your mouth clearly and slowly so that students can see you pronounce the different vowel sounds. They listen and repeat.

Transcript 🔘 1.19
See Student's Book page 20.

2 Allow students time to read the words. Encourage them to say them aloud to themselves, or to each other, to help them decide which of the vowel sounds they are using. Play the recording for students to check their answers.

Transcript 🔘 1.20
See Student's Book page 20.

KEY
/ʌ/ thumb, stomach, cut, son
/əʊ/ toe, phone, throat, wrote
/uː/ tattoo, fruit, boot, tooth

Extension

Whole class: raise your hand and say the word

Assign each student a vowel sound from the pronunciation exercise, so that each vowel sound is represented by roughly one third of the class.

Tell the students to close their books. Say the words from exercise 2 in the pronunciation exercise at random. Students who are that vowel sound should raise their hand and repeat the word. For example, if you say *boot*, students who have the /uː/ sound should raise their hands and say the word. If a student puts up their hand at the wrong time, they are eliminated.

Make the activity more challenging by saying the words more quickly as you go on.

Homework
Workbook p.11 Ex.11
Key p.98

Grammar Check page 21

have/get something *done*

1
Negative: don't have, aren't having, isn't going to have, haven't had
Interrogative: Are you having, Is he going to have, Did we have, Have they had
Short answers negative: don't, aren't, isn't, didn't, haven't past participle

2
1 a   2 b   3 Students' own answers.

3
1 I have/get my hair cut once a month.
2 We have/get our lunch made every day.
3 We had/got our house painted last year.
4 Mike's had/got a tattoo done on his arm.
5 Are you going to have/get your eyes tested?
6 Sarah's having/getting her watch repaired.

4
2 Where's he going to have his MP3 player repaired?
3 When is Mary having some highlights done?
4 Why did you have your photo taken?
5 How often do you have your car serviced?
6 Where have they had a satellite dish installed?

should, ought to

5
1 base form of the verb
2 oughtn't to

6
Students' own answers.

7
give advice

8
1 You'd better pay more attention in class!
2 If I were you. I'd go to the swimming pool.
3 Why don't you phone him?
4 You ought to sleep more.
5 ✓
6 If I were you, I'd go to the gig tonight.

Homework
Workbook p.11 Revision
Key p.98

Skills and culture pages 22–23

1 Speaking

• Students open their books on page 22. Refer them to the questions and allow them time to read through them.

• Working in pairs, students ask and answer the questions. Encourage them to develop their answers and to expand on them by giving reasons for their opinions or by giving examples.

• Monitor, helping out with ideas or vocabulary as necessary. Make a note of any general errors you would like to address at the end of the activity. Put any new vocabulary on the board for the whole class to see.

- At the end of the activity, ask each question from a student or two so that the whole class can hear possible answers.

KEY
Students' own answers.

2 Reading

- Draw students' attention to the title of the text and to the picture on page 23. Explain that we can learn a lot about a text from a title or from pictures that accompany it.
- Students write down three things that they think might be included in the text based on the title. They compare their ideas in pairs.
- Get some feedback from each pair. Put good suggestions on the board for the whole class to see.

KEY
Students' own answers.

3

- Tell students to skim-read the text quickly, reminding them that the aim of a skim-read is to get a general understanding of the text. They check their ideas in exercise 2. Put a tick next to any ideas on the board that are included in the text.

4

- Draw students' attention to the questions and allow them some time to read them. Point out that they should have an idea of the relevant part of the text in which they can find their answer. They should identify key words that will help them focus on a smaller section of the text. In other words, they don't have to read the entire text in detail. Remind them not to spend time worrying about unknown words, as this will slow them down. Instead, they should try to guess the meaning of the word form the context.
- Students answer the questions. They compare their answers in pairs. Check the answers with the whole class.

KEY
1 They have plastic surgery to look more like everyone else.
2 Her teeth were very crooked and her classmates used to make jokes about them.
3 Immediately after the operation, her teeth really hurt, but afterwards she felt much more confident.
4 They sometimes use anabolic steroids and growth hormones.
5 He doesn't want to let others tell him what he should look like and he is proud to be a bit different.
6 It's more important to stay in shape, eat well and try to make the most of ourselves.

5

- Draw students' attention to the highlighted words and expressions in the text. Remind them that instead of using a dictionary, it is quicker and more effective to use the context of an unknown word or expression to work out its meaning.
- Students match the words to their synonyms or definitions. They check their answers in pairs. Check answers as a class.

KEY
1 crooked   2 self-esteem   3 recover
4 stay in shape   5 stand out   6 Whereas
7 eating disorders   8 pressure   9 miserable
10 despite

6 Listening

- Tell students they are going to listen to Amar interviewing a yoga teacher. In pairs, allow students one or two minutes to think of anything they know about yoga. Get some feedback from each pair.
- Allow students time to read the first statement. Explain that they have to identify whether the statement is true or false. Play the recording until the // symbol. Ask the students where yoga comes from and elicit that it comes from India. Therefore the first statement is false.
- Allow the students time to read the rest of the statements, reminding them to identify keywords that will help them find the answers. Play the recording from the beginning. Students decide if the sentences are true or false. They check their answers in pairs.
- Play the recording a second time. Check answers as a class. Ask students to compare the information in the interview with their ideas about yoga before they listened.

Transcript 🔘 1.21
Amar First of all, could you explain what yoga is?
Kate Yoga comes from India and it's a system of exercises which help to control the body and the mind. //
Amar Do you think yoga could be useful for teenagers?
Kate Definitely. Yoga is very good for young people. Physically, it increases flexibility, strength and coordination. You improve your concentration when you practise asanas, which are the positions, and through breathing techniques. Yoga really helps you to feel calm and relaxed.
Amar In your opinion, is stress a problem for teenagers?
Kate Well, they live in a 'fast' world of busy parents, school pressures, noisy, crowded shopping centres and clubs. They play a lot of video games that put them in situations that can make them quite anxious or tense. We don't usually think of these things as stressful, but they often are.
Amar Would you recommend yoga for shy or insecure teenagers?
Kate Yes, I would. When you do yoga you learn that your body can do amazing things and you learn to appreciate it and gradually stop being so critical of yourself. Doing yoga helps teenagers to accept themselves and it makes them more confident. They realise that they are unique, special individuals.
Amar Why do you think teenagers like it?
Kate Mostly, I think, because they soon realise that it's good for them and that it's a good way to feel better inside. And the exercise helps them look better on the outside, too!

KEY
1 F: Yoga comes from India.
2 F: It is definitely suitable.
3 F: It increases strength.
4 T.
5 T.
6 F: You gradually stop being so critical of yourself.
7 T.
8 T.

7 Writing

- Remind students about James' problem in the reading text on page 22. Ask the class how they would feel if they were James and elicit a few ideas from one or two students.

- Read the instructions with the class and go through the prompts with the students. Point out that they should include this information in their email, but that they should link it together in a natural way. In other words, the email should not consist of three separated pieces of information, but should flow together.

- Have a quick brainstorming session with the class about what information they could include in their email. Remind them that an email (especially an email to a friend) will be informal and that they can use informal features such as contraction and phrasal verbs. If you feel it's necessary, remind them of the structure of an email.

- Students write the email for homework.

Extension
Language plus p.88

Language review pages 24–25

Vocabulary

1
1 does 2 pitch 3 do 4 kick 5 courts 6 fit
7 arts 8 does 9 sporty 10 doing

2
a 1, 3, 4, 2
b 4, 1, 3, 2
c 3, 1, 2, 4
d 2, 3, 1, 4
1 b 2 c 3 d 4 a

3
Possible answers:
2 My shoulder hurts.
3 I've got stomach ache.
4 I've got a sore throat.
5 I've injured my knees.
6 I've got a bad cough.

4
Students' own answers.

Grammar

5
Across
4 thumb 5 should 9 painkillers 11 done
12 pierced 13 ought
Down
1 vitamin 3 taken 6 had 7 lips 8 better 10 wrist
11 dyed 14 get

6
1 losing 2 to go 3 drinking 4 walking 5 doing
6 to walk

7
1 …primary school did you use to go to?
2 …did you use to go to primary school?
3 …did your dad use to live when he was a boy?
4 …did your mum use to get up when you were a child?
5 …did you use to play when you were younger?

8
- Students listen to the recording to check their answers in exercise 7.

Transcript 1.22
See Student's Book page 25, exercise 7 and Key.

9
Students' own answers.

10
Students' own answers.

11
Students' own answers.

12
1 Michael plays tennis very well.
2 William runs pretty slowly.
3 Rob swims fast.
4 Mary drives very carefully.
5 I speak English fluently.

Communication

13
Students' own answers.

14
1 in 2 out 3 make 4 take 5 a 6 on 7 get
8 on

Extra Practice
CD-ROM

Topic and vocabulary

Emotions

Wishes

Feelings

TV reality shows

Mind games

Grammar

Second conditional

wish + Past simple

make + object + adjective/verb

Functions

Imagining different situations

Making wishes

Talking about feelings

Skills and culture/pronunciation

Speaking: conversation

Reading: predicting content, matching photos to information, true or false

Listening: listening for general understanding, multiple matching

Writing: a summary

Pronunciation: *you* + vowel sound

Estimated time: 7–8 hours

How would you feel if…? pages 26–27

Warm-up

- Put the following words on the board: *sad, happy, bored, excited,* and elicit that they are adjectives to describe emotions. In pairs, students have two minutes to think of a situation where they might feel these emotions.

- Get some feedback from a few pairs, putting any new vocabulary on the board. Ask the class which of the adjectives are negative (sad, happy) and which of them are positive (happy, excited).

1 Vocabulary • emotions

- Refer students to page 26 and to the list of emotion adjectives in the box. Explain the task and tell them not to worry about any unknown words just yet, but to focus on the adjectives that they already know.

- Monitor, helping out as necessary. When students are ready, they compare their lists in pairs, helping each other complete the columns where they can. Check answers as a class, checking for understanding as you do so.

KEY

positive: laid-back, confident, relieved, happy, excited

negative: envious, depressed, embarrassed, annoyed, worried, uneasy, angry, scared, upset, jealous, bored

Extension

Pairwork: When was the last time you felt…?

Students work in pairs. Tell them to think about the last time they felt the emotions in exercise 1. Encourage them to explain why they felt like this. For example, *The last time I felt bored was last Tuesday. I was on the train and I didn't have anything to read or any music to listen to.*

Monitor the students as they work, making sure they are using the adjectives correctly.

2 What would I do?

- Draw students' attention to the photo of Lisa and ask them what they think she is reading. Elicit that it looks like she is reading a magazine. Ask the students if any of them like reading magazines and accept any answers. Encourage them to explain why they like/don't like magazines.

- Refer the students to the quiz and ask them if they have ever done a personality quiz. Get brief feedback.

- Play the recording. Students follow the quiz and listen as Lisa answers the questions, circling the options she chooses. Check answers as a class.

- Students do the quiz about themselves. Alternatively, to encourage speaking practice, ask the students to do the quiz in pairs, interviewing each other. Monitor, helping out where necessary.

- When they finish, refer them to page 111 for their scores. Get some feedback from a few students about their scores. Do they agree with their results?

Transcript 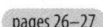 1.23

Lisa Oh , this looks interesting… 'Try the TeenAge Personality Quiz and find out what sort of person you really are!' Well, let's see!

Number 1: 'If I went to a party alone, I'd feel a) a bit scared. b) really bored. c) laid-back and confident.' Hmm… I suppose I'd be a tiny bit nervous at first if I didn't know anyone, but not scared. I think c) for that one. Yes, I'm quite confident really.

Number 2: 'If my friend won the lottery, I'd feel a) happy for him or her. b) a bit envious. c) angry that it wasn't me.' Hmm… I should be happy but I think I might be a bit envious, so that's b). Maybe if it was a good friend they'd give me some of the money!

OK, number 3: 'If a friend borrowed my bike and had an accident, a) I'd feel worried about my friend. b) I'd feel annoyed about my bike. c) I wouldn't care. Accidents happen!' I suppose I might be a bit annoyed about my bike if they completely destroyed it, but mostly I'd be worried about my friend, so a).

Number 4: 'If a close friend of mine got very ill, I'd feel a) relieved it wasn't me. b) very worried. c) depressed.' I'd definitely be really worried about them. How horrible! I'd only be relieved when they got better!

What's number 5? 'If I arranged to meet a friend at a club and she didn't come, a) I'd feel very angry. b) I'd feel worried about her. c) I wouldn't be upset.' Hmm… This one's more

difficult. I think my friends would phone me if they weren't coming, so I don't think this would happen, but if I was all on my own at the club I think I might be a bit angry. Yes, a).
Number 6: 'If I had an exam tomorrow, I'd feel a) relaxed. b) excited. c) nervous.' What? Definitely c) for this one – I've never felt excited about an exam! And I never feel relaxed until I get the results and see I've passed!
Number 7: 'If they invited me to appear on a TV quiz show, I'd feel a) excited. b) embarrassed. c) very nervous.' Oh, I don't think I'd be nervous – I'd be too excited about being on TV! Definitely a)!
So, the last one's number 8: 'If I saw news of a terrible natural disaster on TV, a) I wouldn't care. Disasters happen all the time. b) I'd feel depressed. What a tragedy! c) I'd feel relieved. At least it wasn't in my country!' Oh dear, I don't know… I would definitely care, but I think if I was really honest I'd have to say c)! I hope nothing awful happens at home while I'm here!
So, let's see what it says about my personality…

KEY
1 c   2 b   3 a   4 b   5 a   6 c   7 a   8 c
Students' own answers.

Grammar Guide • Second conditional

- Check the students' understanding of the structure and use of the affirmative, negative and interrogative forms of the Second conditional. Point out that there are two clauses in the sentence and emphasise that the *if* clause takes the Past simple while the consequence clause takes *would*.

- Explain that the second conditional refers to an imaginary situation in the present or future: we are talking about what we *would do* or what *would happen*. There is a slight possibility these things could really happen, but it is very unlikely.

LOOK OUT!

1 Make sure that students understand the use of the comma in conditional sentences. Explain that the two clauses can be swapped around, but that we only use a comma when the *if* clause comes first.

2 Explain that *could* and *might* can be used instead of *would*. *Could* means that we're talking about the ability to do something while *might* makes is less strong than *would*, i.e. we are not sure about what we would do in a situation.

---

3 Check!

- Students complete the sentences with the correct form of the verbs in the box. If it is a weaker class, ask them to match the correct verbs to the correct sentences first before they complete the task.

- When they have finished, they check their answers in pairs. Check answers as a class.

KEY
1 went…would visit   2 saw…would be
3 would buy…won   4 would live…spoke
5 knew…would kill   6 found…would scream

Extension

Pair work: If money grew on trees, …
Write the following *if* clauses on the board:
If money grew on trees, …
If animals could speak, …
If the world were flat, …
If I could travel to the past, …
If school didn't exist, …
Working in pairs, students think of a suitable imaginary ending for each one. Make sure they use *would* and the base form of the verb. Monitor, helping out as necessary and putting any new vocabulary on the board for the class to see. When students have finished, ask each pair to read out their sentences. Have a vote on the funniest pair.

4 What if…?

- Put the following sentence on the board: *If I won €1,000, I'd go on a nice holiday.* Ask the class if they would do the same thing and get brief feedback.

- Then, write the following on the board: *If I went on a long trip around the world…* Ask the class for a suitable ending and complete the sentence with their ideas. Elicit that you are creating a new conditional sentence using the second clause of the previous sentence.

- Draw students' attention to the six pictures. In their pairs, they think about what is happening to Lucy. At this stage, don't make them do the full task – just ask them to follow the story. Monitor, helping out where necessary.

- When students are ready, bring them back to the first picture and divide them into A/B pairs. Point out the words below the picture and explain the task. Student A begins with picture 1, then student B continues with the picture 2 using the second clause from student A's sentence. They then continue with the rest of the pictures until they have a complete story.

- Check answers as a class. Choose one student at random and ask them to read the first sentence. Then choose five more students to read out the other five sentences, correcting any mistakes as necessary.

- Ask students to close their books and repeat the activity, with the students saying the sentences from memory.

KEY
2 If she went to the USA next summer, she'd stay with her cousin Jason.
3 If she stayed with her cousin Jason, she'd go out with his friends.
4 If she went out with his friends, she'd find a new boyfriend.
5 If she found a new boyfriend, she'd fall in love.
6 If she fell in love, she wouldn't want to come home.

5 What would you do?

- Refer students to the first clauses of conditional sentences and allow them time to read through them. Explain that they are going to hear a person in each situation and that they have to complete what that person would do.

- Do the first one as an example. Play the recording until the // symbol. Ask the students what the woman does and elicit that she screams. Therefore they complete the sentence with *I'd scream*. Then play the rest of the first sentence for students to check the sentence. Continue in this way with the remaining sentences, checking the answers as you go.

- Tell students to complete the sentences so they are true for themselves. Monitor, helping out as necessary. Ask them to compare their sentences in pairs.

Transcript 🎧 1.24

1

Woman What's that in the bath? Oh no, it's a huge spider – aaaarghh! //
If I found a spider in the bath, I'd scream.

2

Boy Hey! What are you doing in my living room? … Hello, is that the police? There's been a burglary…
If I found a strange man in my house, I'd call the police.

3

Girl If I fell off my bike, I'd go to the hospital.

4

Man Oh wow! Hooray! I've won the lottery! Now I can go to Jamaica!
If I won the lottery, I'd go and live in Jamaica.

5

Girl Hey! Are you Elijah Wood?
Elijah Yes, that's right!
Girl Would you like to have a coffee with me?
Elijah Sure! Why not?
Girl If I met Elijah Wood, I'd invite him to have a coffee with me.

6

Vicar Do you, Judd O'Connor, take Alison Hodges to be your lawful wedded wife?
Man I do…
If I got married, I'd invite lots of friends to a big party.

KEY

1 …I'd scream
2 …I'd call the police.
3 …I'd go to the hospital.
4 …I'd go and live in Jamaica.
5 …I'd invite him to have a coffee with me.
6 …I'd invite lots of friends to a big party.

Extension

Group work: personality quiz

Students work in groups of three. Refer them to the quiz that Lisa did on page 26 and tell them they are going to make a similar quiz themselves. Encourage them to make five questions and to create their own situations and possible options.

Monitor, helping out as necessary. When students have finished, divide the class into pairs so that each pair has two members from different groups. They interview each other with their quizzes.

Homework
Workbook pp.14–15 Ex.1–6
Key pp.98–99

I wish I wasn't on my own… 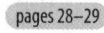 pages 28–29

Warm-up

- Write *If I had to celebrate my birthday alone,…* on the board. Ask students to complete it using any of the adjectives from page 26. They compare their ideas in pairs.
- Get some feedback from each pair.

6

- Refer students to the photos and ask them what is happening. Elicit that it is Jackie's birthday. Ask them how she looks in the first photo and elicit that she looks miserable or depressed.
- Play the recording. Students listen and read the text.

Transcript 🎧 1.25

See Student's Book page 28.

LEARN IT! USE IT! TRANSLATE IT! Remind the students of these expressions in the dialogue. Check understanding by asking them to give you the equivalent expressions in their language.

7 Comprehension check

- Students read the text again and decide if the sentences are true or false, correcting the false ones. They check their answers in pairs. Check answers as a class.
- Ask the students if Jackie's wish came true and elicit that it did because Amar and Steve arrived.

KEY

1 F: Jackie is celebrating her birthday in London with her aunt.
2 T.
3 F: She didn't know that they were coming. She was surprised.
4 T.
5 T.

Grammar Guide • *wish* + Past simple

- Remind students about Jackie and ask them if she is in Wales. Elicit that she isn't in Wales and write this on the board: *Jackie isn't in Wales*. Ask them to look at the first photo and draw their attention to the sentence *I wish I was in Wales*. Ask them what it means and elicit that Jackie is expressing regret. She is saying where she would like to be now. She would like the situation to be different.
- Make sure students understand that *wish* is hypothetical. Although we use the Past simple after *wish,* we are referring to the present (the imaginary present). This can be confusing, so be as clear as possible.
- Highlight the change from Present simple negative to Past simple affirmative, and explain that we must always switch from positive to negative or negative to positive to make wishes.
- Check that students understand the affirmative, negative and interrogative structures. Point out that we can use either *was* or *were* for the third person singular form of *be*.

8 Check!

- Students complete the sentences with a suitable verb. If necessary, help them identify the verbs that they will need before they choose the correct form. They check answers in pairs. Check answers as a class.

KEY

1 wasn't/weren't 2 had 3 didn't have 4 was/were
5 lived 6 wasn't/weren't 7 had 8 played

9 I wish I was more exciting!

- Students work in pairs. Draw their attention to the first picture and ask them what they see. Elicit that there is a single boy looking at a couple kissing. Ask the class how they think he feels and elicit that he might feel jealous or miserable.

- Tell students to look at the remaining pictures in their pairs. Encourage them to imagine what each person is feeling and why.

- When they are ready, play the recording. They match each wish with the correct picture and check their answers in pairs. Check answers as a class.

- Play the recording a second time, pausing to allow students to write down the wishes. Check their answers as a class by choosing a different student to read out each wish.

- In pairs, students look back at the pictures and try to remember the wishes without looking at their sentences. Monitor, listening out for correct use of *wish*.

Transcript 🔘 1.26

1 I wish I was a film star.
2 I wish I was older.
3 I wish I wasn't so bad at tennis.
4 I wish I didn't have an exam.
5 I wish I was a Formula 1 champion.
6 I wish I had a girlfriend.

KEY

A 6 B 4 C 5 D 1 E 3 F 2

Extensions

Individual work: facts to wishes…

Think of five everyday situations you can say to the class. They should all be in the present. For example, *It's raining. I'm feeling very ill. My brother is smarter than I am. I don't have enough money to buy new clothes. I don't understand English grammar.*

Say each sentence to the class and allow them time to write down the equivalent wish. When they have finished, they check their wishes in pairs. Check as a class.

Individual work: wishes to facts…

Think of five wishes you can say to the class. They should all use the Past simple. For example, *I wish I were tall and thin. I wish it were my birthday every day. I wish I could speak five languages. I wish school didn't exist. I wish I could find a magic lamp.*

Say each wish to the class and allow them time to write down the equivalent present fact. When they have finished, they check their facts in pairs. Check as a class.

---

10 Whose wish is it?

- Read the task with the whole class and make sure they understand what they are going to do. Divide them into small groups of three or four.

- Each student writes three wishes. Monitor, helping out as necessary and making sure they are forming the sentences correctly. They mix up their wishes and then choose from them at random to guess who wrote each wish.

- Encourage them to explain to the other students why they wrote their wishes. Monitor, listening out for correct use of *wish* and making a note of any errors to come back to later.

- Get some feedback from each group about the wishes that they made. Have a vote on the three best/funniest wishes in the class. (Pay attention to any sensitive issues that come up in the wishes – keep the activity light-hearted but avoid offence. Teenagers can be very sensitive about themselves.)

KEY
Students' own answers.

ALREADY FINISHED? Students imagine what their teacher would wish about them. Get feedback from them and reinforce the activity by telling them three wishes of your own.

Homework
Workbook pp.16 Ex.7–8
Key p.99

Talking about feelings   page 30

11 They make me feel nervous!

- Draw students' attention to the photo and ask them what they see. Elicit that it is a photo of a theatre. Ask the class how they would feel if they were going to the theatre this evening (remind them of the emotion adjectives on page 26). Elicit any acceptable answers.

- Explain the task and allow students time to read through the sentences. When they are ready, play the recording. Students choose the correct alternatives. Check answers as a class.

- Ask the students to briefly discuss in their pairs how they would feel if the hypnotist chose them. Get some feedback, encouraging students to use the second conditional, i.e. *If the hypnotist chose me, I'd feel…*

Transcript 🔘 1.27

Jackie Wasn't it lovely of my aunt to get us tickets for Michael Morton? It'll be great!
Steve Yes… I love going to shows like this. I'm really excited. I've heard a lot about Michael Morton but I've never seen him live.
Amar I'm not so sure. He's a hypnotist – I think I prefer magicians.
Steve Really? I don't.
Amar Yes, it's because hypnotists make me feel nervous.
Jackie Why?
Amar I'm afraid they'll make me do something stupid.
Steve OK, I see what you mean. But it's pretty unlikely that he'll choose you. I mean there are hundreds of people here.
Jackie Yeah… don't worry, Amar.
Steve Here we are. These are our seats.

Jackie Fantastic! Right in the front row.

Michael Now, ladies and gentlemen. Welcome to my show, where through the power of hypnosis I'll make normal people do the strangest things! It might make you feel uneasy, it might make you feel embarrassed, but it certainly won't make you feel bored! Right, first of all I need a volunteer from the audience. How about you, sir? The young man in the front row.

Amar Who? Me?

Jackie Go on, Amar! He wants you!

Michael Yes, you sir! Step this way, please. Now don't be afraid!

Amar Oh no!

KEY

1 excited   2 hasn't   3 hypnotist   4 nervous   5 front
6 Amar

> **LANGUAGE TIP** Explain that we can use *make* to describe how we feel or what we do as a result of something else. For example, *Rain makes me depressed.* (I am depressed because of the rain) or *Funny films make me laugh.* (I laugh because of funny films).
>
> Point out that, in this context, *make* is always followed by a direct object and then either a verb or an adjective.

Pronunciation • *you* + vowel sound

Write *a, e, i, o* and *u* on the board. Elicit that these are vowels. Write *you* on the board and ask the students to repeat it. Elicit that it sounds like a vowel and explain that when *you* is followed by a word beginning with a vowel, we link them together.

1 Play the recording and pause. Repeat the sentence yourself and ask the students to repeat. Now repeat *you anxious* nice and slowly so that the class can hear you link them together. Ask them to repeat this.

Transcript 1.28

See Student's Book page 30.

2 Allow students time to read the sentences. Encourage them to say them aloud to themselves, or to each other, to practise linking the vowel sounds together. Play the recording, pausing after each sentence to allow students time to repeat. Repeat the sentences yourself to reinforce the examples on the recording.

Transcript 1.29

See Student's Book page 30.

12 How does it make you feel?

- Refer students to the photos and ask them to look through them. Tell them to choose any five and to choose an adjective to describe their feelings in each of them. Monitor, helping out where necessary.

- When students are ready, they work in pairs. Refer them to the example and point out the structure of the question and the answer. In their pairs, they ask and answer questions about the pictures they have chosen.

- Monitor the students, listening out for correct use of *make*. At the end of the activity, get some feedback from a few pairs by asking a student to describe how their partner feels in different situations.

KEY
Students' own answers.

> **Extension**
>
> ### Pair work: If I stood on top of tall buildings, …
>
> Refer students back to the pictures. Ask them to work in pairs and to make a Second conditional sentence for each picture. The first clause should consist of the prompts, while the second clause should be their own idea. For example, *If I stood on top of fall buildings, I'd get dizzy and fall down.*
>
> Monitor the students as they speak, listening out for correct use of the Second conditional.

ALREADY FINISHED? Read the instructions with the students and check for understanding. They write their paragraphs describing what scares them, including the points that are suggested. You could also set this activity for homework.

Homework
Workbook p.16–17 Ex.9–10
Key p.99

Grammar Check page 31

Second conditional

1
Past simple
Subject…subject

2
1 would   2 was or were   3 an improbable or impossible

3
1 …if I had a car.
2 If they were English, …
3 …I'd study it at university.
4 …if I had his email address.
5 What would you do…
6 If I could go out with an actor, …
7 If I wasn't/weren't ill, …
8 …I'd scream!

4
1 c   2 e   3 f   4 b   5 d   6 a

wish + Past simple

5
present

6
1 I wish I had a brother.
2 Adam wishes he didn't have an exam tomorrow.
3 I wish I wasn't/weren't scared of heights.
4 He wishes he knew her.
5 We wish we were on holiday.
6 I wish I spoke Spanish.
7 I wish I could play the guitar.
8 I wish I spent less on phone calls.

7

1 I wish I weren't so shy.
2 Jan wishes she could play volleyball well.
3 I wish I had blonde hair.
4 He wishes that he was taller.
5 They wished they lived in a bigger house.
6 I wish I wasn't so depressed.
7 I wish that I understood the answer.
8 We wish our teacher gave us better marks.

make + object + adjective/verb

8
Students' own answers.

> **Homework**
> **Workbook p.17 Revision**
> **Key p.99**

Skills and culture   pages 32–33

Warm-up

• Ask the class if they remember what kind of show Amar, Jackie and Steve went to see. Elicit that they went to see a hypnotist.

• In pairs, tell students they have about two minutes to decide if they believe in hypnotism or magic. Get feedback from a few pairs. Encourage them to explain their opinions.

1 Speaking

• Divide students into A/B pairs. Students A turn to page 111 and students B open their books on page 32. Explain that students A have to read the instructions they have to students B, while students B follow them.

• Monitor the students during this activity, making sure the students are following the steps correctly.

• Ask each student B to raise their hand if student A guessed their planet correctly. (NB They all will, if they followed the steps correctly)

• When students have finished, refer them to the questions on page 32. In their pairs, they discuss the questions. Monitor, helping out where necessary and reminding them to look out for the questions using *make* and the Second conditional. Encourage them to expand on their answers by giving reasons or examples.

• At the end of the activity, get feedback on each question from a pair or two. Does the rest of the class agree?

KEY
Students' own answers.

2 Reading

• Draw students' attention to the photos at the bottom of the page and ask them to discuss the question in pairs.

• Get some feedback from each pair. Put good suggestions on the board for the whole class to see.

KEY
Students' own answers.

3

• Tell students to skim-read the text quickly, reminding them that the aim of a skim-read is to get a general understanding of the text. Ask them to underline any sentence they think might describe the photos in the previous exercise. Were any of them right?

KEY
Students' own answers.

4

• Draw students' attention to the statements and allow them some time to read them. Point out that they should have an idea of the relevant part of the text in which they can find their answer. They should identify key words that will help them focus on a smaller section of the text, so that they don't have to read the entire text in detail for every statement. Remind them not to spend time worrying about unknown words, as this will just slow them down.

• Students choose true or false. They compare their answers in pairs. Check the answers with the whole class. Ask them to correct the false sentences.

KEY
1 F: Derren Brown said he would make business managers steal some money.
2 F: They thought they were taking part in motivational seminars.
3 F: He gave them a toy gun.
4 T.
5 T.
6 F: One manager didn't take the money.
7 F: They were amazed by the programme, but there was a lot of controversy about the effect it might have.

5 Vocabulary

• Draw students' attention to the highlighted words and expressions in the text. At this stage they should be used to guessing the meanings of words from their context in a sentence, but remind them anyway.

• Students match the words to their synonyms or definitions. They check their answers in pairs. Check answers as a class.

KEY
1 intense   2 techniques   3 realising   4 ordinary
5 obedient   6 participants   7 controversy
8 fascinating   9 participating   10 associate

6 Listening

• Ask the students what they think about Derren Brown's programme. In pairs, they discuss their ideas briefly. Get some feedback from a few pairs.

• Explain the task and refer them to the question. Play the recording. Students identify who has more doubts about Derren Brown and his show.

• Refer students to the statements and allow them time to read them and explain that they are going to listen to the recording again. They should underline key words in each statement that will help them locate the answer in the recording.

• Play the recording a second time. Students choose Alistair or Jasmine for each statement. Check answers as a class.

Transcript 🔊 1.30

Alistair Did you see Derren Brown on TV last night?

Jasmine Yes, I did.

Alistair It was fantastic, wasn't it?

Jasmine Well, I don't know… People like him make me feel a bit anxious. I don't trust them.

Alistair Oh, I don't think I'd say that, but I think I know what you mean. He sort of… manipulates people.

Jasmine Yes, that's right. I don't really think it's right to get people to do things they don't really want to do.

Alistair Yes, I suppose so. If they asked you to go on one of his shows, would you accept? I'm not sure.

Jasmine I definitely wouldn't. I really didn't like it when he got those people to do a robbery.

Alistair No. I mean, it's a bit dangerous to show that it's possible to get people to do something like that. I mean, if someone copied him, maybe they'd be able to make people rob a real bank.

Jasmine But some of his shows are brilliant.

Alistair Yeah, I liked it when he was talking to that man at Waterloo Station and he managed to take his watch and wallet and then his tie! He was just talking to him, and then he asked him for them, and the man just gave them to him! If a total stranger asked you for your wallet, would you give it to him? I couldn't believe it! How on earth does he do it? I wish I knew! It's incredible.

Jasmine Mmm… Yes, that show was great. But some of the stuff he does really makes me feel uneasy.

Alistair Mmm… but it's fascinating to watch!

KEY

Jasmine has more doubts.

1 A   2 J   3 J   4 A   5 A   6 A

> **STUDY STRATEGY** Ask the students what a summary is and elicit that it is a shorter version of a longer text that only includes the most important ideas or points.
>
> Read through the steps for writing a good summary with the class. Emphasise that they should try to use their own words when they make notes on the main facts and that they should write their summary based on these notes. This reduces the risk of copying parts of the text and is a useful skill to develop. Remind them that linking words are necessary so that the facts can be joined together to make the text flow naturally.

7 Writing

- Read the *Study Strategy* with the class. Tell them to slowly read the text in exercise 2 again and to identify what they think are the most important facts in it. Ask them to compare their ideas in pairs and get some feedback.

- Students write a summary of the text. Point out that they should stick to the word limit and that they should leave some time to check their summary for grammar or spelling mistakes. This activity can be set for homework.

Extension
Language plus p.90

Exam plus 3

Objectives
To practise exams related to the material covered in Unit 3
Use of English: Multiple-choice cloze
Speaking: Picture-based discussion
Listening: Sentence completion

Use of English • Multiple-choice cloze

page 34

Warm-up

- Tell the class how you like to relax (you don't have to be honest!), for example, *When I want to relax, I go to a quiet place and read a good book. Sometimes, I listen to relaxing music on my MP3 player while I read.*

- Working in pairs, students tell each other their favourite way to relax. After about two minutes, stop the class and get some feedback from a few pairs. Have a quick vote on who relaxes in the best way.

1

- Ask the class what they think is the opposite of feeling relaxed and elicit that it is feeling stressed. Ask them to suggest a few situations that might make them feel stressed and put their ideas on the board.

- Refer them to the text and tell them to read it quickly, ignoring the gaps. Ask them whether the text says that stress is a good thing or a bad thing. Elicit that it says stress can be both good and bad.

- Read the instructions with the class and draw their attention to the multiple-choice options 1–10. Make sure they understand that only one of the options is possible in each gap. Point out that they must think carefully about the words around the gap so that they make the correct choice.

- Do the first question together as an example. Read the first two sentences and elicit that the author is describing the reasons for being stressed. Read the options for the first gap and elicit that *c* is the correct answer because *changes* is a plural noun. Options *a* and *c* are incorrect because they are singular and do not grammatically fit in the gap. Option *d* is incorrect because *them* is a pronoun.

- Students complete the rest of the task by themselves and check their answers in pairs. Check their answers as a class, explaining in each case why the other options are incorrect.

KEY

1 c   2 d   3 b   4 a   5 a   6 b   7 c   8 a

> **EXAM TIP** Point out that students should try to eliminate incorrect answers if they don't know the correct answer. This reduces possibilities and can make it easier for them to arrive at the correct answer. They should never leave an empty gap.

Speaking • Picture-based discussion page 109

2

- Tell students to turn to page 109 and draw their attention to the three pictures on the right. Ask them what they can see and elicit a brief description of each photo from the class.
- Read the instructions with the class and read through the prompts with them. Make sure they understand what they have to do.
- Remind them that they are going to use the photos along with the prompts to discuss what they think about the different things people do to change their appearance. Remind them not to simply answer the prompts directly but to use them to support the discussion.
- Divide students into small groups of three or four and tell them to start the task. Monitor the students as they discuss. Make a note of any general errors students make to go over at the end of the activity, and observe how they link their ideas together. Try not to interrupt the students too much in their discussion.
- When students have finished, get some feedback from each group about the main ideas they discussed. If you like, and if the students are able, you could bring the discussion to a class level for a few minutes to end the activity.

Functions bank
Workbook p.51

Listening • Sentence completion page 34

Warm-up

- Ask the students if they know anyone who has changed their appearance by having a tattoo, a piercing or their hair dyed. They briefly discuss the question in pairs.
- Get feedback from a few pairs.

3

- Read the instructions carefully with the students and make sure they understand the task. There will be two people interviewed and they will be asked the same questions. Emphasise that they only need one or two words to complete each of the statements.
- Allow students time to read the incomplete statements. Point out that as they read them, they should think about what the missing word could be. Will they need a verb, noun or an adjective in each case?
- Remind them to underline key words. This will help them to focus as they listen and they will be able to better identify the relevant section of the recording.
- Explain that they will hear the recording twice. When they listen for the first time, they should familiarise themselves with the dialogue and match each sentence to a relevant part of it. If they are able to, they should note down possible answers. Emphasise that if they don't identify the correct answer on the first listening, they shouldn't worry as they will hear the recording a second time.
- Do the first sentence as an example with the class. Elicit that the students need a noun (probably a part of the body) to complete the sentence and play the recording until the // symbol in the transcript. Allow students

time to make a note of their answers and play the same segment a second time. Elicit that the correct answer is *ears*.

- When students are ready, explain that they are going to do the rest of the task by themselves. Play the recording from the beginning.
- Allow students to compare their answers/possible answers in pairs. Explain that when they listen for the second time, they should listen carefully to check their answers. If they didn't identify an answer during the first listening, explain that they should be able to identify it more easily during the second listening, as they are more familiar with the dialogue.
- Play the recording again and check answers as a class. If you feel it is necessary, play the recording a third time and pause after each of the relevant sections as you check their answers.

Transcript 1.31

Anne Hi, Nathan. I'd like to ask you some questions about body art.

Nathan Fine.

Anne First of all, how do you feel about piercing? Would you have your ears or nose pierced, for example?

Nathan Well, I suppose I might have an ear pierced. Some of my mates have had it done and I suppose it's quite trendy at the moment. //

Anne And what about tattoos? Have you ever thought of having a tattoo done?

Nathan Er, no. I don't really like the idea. I mean, it's very painful. Then, if you change your mind about the tattoo, it's very expensive and even more painful to have it removed.

Anne And what about cosmetic surgery? Would you have that done?

Nathan Erm… I don't think I'd do it personally, but I can understand why some people do it. If you really don't like a part of your body, then I think it's OK if you want to change it. But again it's very expensive – and risky.

Anne What about having your hair dyed an unusual colour?

Nathan What, like bright orange, or something?

Anne Yes, that sort of thing.

Nathan I don't think that's really me. I think I'd look a right idiot with orange hair.

Anne Thanks for answering my questions, Nathan….Hello, Virginia. Now, you heard the questions I asked Nathan. I'd like to hear your answers to the same questions.

Virginia OK.

Anne First, what about body piercing? You know, having your belly button or your ear pierced.

Virginia Well, as you can see, I've had my ears pierced twice and look, I've also got a diamond in my belly button.

Anne Oh, yes. And what about a tattoo? Have you ever had a tattoo done?

Virginia No, I'm too young. But I'd like to have one when I'm 18.

Anne What sort of tattoo and where?

Virginia I don't know – something simple like a flower and somewhere not immediately visible, like on my shoulder or back, because I think people associate tattoos with a certain type of person. Also, when you get older, you might not want to show it any more.

Anne And how do you feel about cosmetic surgery?

Virginia Well, I don't really like the idea. I mean, any sort of surgery is potentially dangerous, so it seems stupid to take a risk when it's not really necessary. I think people are too worried about image and being perfect. Nobody's perfect, and even beautiful people aren't always satisfied.

Anne Even when someone has a complex about it?

Virginia I think you have to try to accept how you are.

Anne And finally, what about having your hair dyed an unusual colour?

Virginia Yes, I did that once. It wasn't very popular with my parents or my teachers at school, though.

Anne What colour?

Virginia Well, I had my hair dyed blue, but I got bored with it after a couple of weeks. It was a bit of a shock seeing myself in the mirror in the morning. I don't think I'd do it again – well, not blue anyway.

Anne Thanks, Virginia.

KEY

1 ears   2 painful   3 change   4 unusual   5 some/two
6 older   7 necessary   8 teachers

> **EXAM TIP** Emphasise the importance of identifying what type of word is needed in each statement. The missing word must not only make sense logically, but must fit grammatically too.

Further exam practice
Workbook pp.22–23

Exam plus 4

> **Objectives**
> To practise exams related to the material covered in Unit 4
> **Reading:** Multiple matching
> **Writing:** Informal letter

Reading • Multiple matching page 35

Warm-up

- Write *true love* on the board and ask the students to discuss in small groups whether they believe in it or not. Allow them about three or four minutes to exchange opinions and encourage them to explain them.
- Get brief feedback from each group. What do the majority of the class think?

1

- Draw students' attention to the text, explaining that there are seven opinions on true love. Remind them that they should first skim-read the text to get a general understanding. Ask students to skim-read all the paragraphs and to write one or two words beside each of them that summarises what they read. It doesn't have to be perfectly accurate, just a rough summary of what the opinion of each person is.
- Ask them to compare their summaries in pairs. Get feedback from a few pairs.
- Explain the task and draw their attention to the opinions 1–5. Point out that they have to match each opinion with a paragraph, and that there are two paragraphs they do not need.
- As they have now done a skim-read, they have a rough idea of what each paragraph says so the task should be easier. Do the first one together as a class.
- Read the first statement and elicit that they need to match it with a paragraph where somebody likes being in love and doesn't think single people can be happy. Therefore, they should probably focus on paragraphs with a generally positive view on love and look for synonyms to identify the correct one. Allow them a few minutes to decide and elicit that the correct answer is paragraph B.
- Students do the remaining opinions by themselves and check their answers in pairs. Check answers as a class, explaining why each answer is correct.

KEY

1 B   2 A   3 G   4 D   5 C

> **EXAM TIP** Stress the importance, once again, of a skim-read before doing the task as it really does help in focussing on the relevant part of the text. In this type of task, it's important to be able to identify synonyms that will link the statement with the right paragraph.

Writing • Informal letter page 35

2

- Refer students to the extract from the letter and ask them to read it quickly to find out what Joe's problem is. Elicit that he's too shy to ask a girl out because he doesn't want to make a fool of himself.

- Read the instructions with the students and make sure they understand what is required. Remind students of the structure and features of an informal letter and refer them to page 102 to refresh their memories.

- Point out that it is always a good idea to make a plan before they write. Allow them some time to think about what they are going to say and encourage them to make some notes. They should include the information suggested in the prompts, but point out that they should develop this with their own ideas.

- Allow students about 20–25 minutes to write the letter. Remind them that they should always leave some time at the end of a writing activity to read what they've written to check for mistakes.

> **EXAM TIP** Remind students that as informal writing is similar to the way we speak, it is easy to lose track, as it is less structured than formal writing. Remind students that they need to focus on the four pieces of information instead of taking up space with unnecessary information.

Further exam practice
Workbook pp.22–23

Topic and vocabulary
The European Union

Relationships

Dating customs in the past and present

Grammar
Question tags

Past perfect

Phrasal verbs

Reported speech · *say, tell*

Functions
Checking information

Describing events

Reporting statements

Skills and culture/pronunciation
Listening: comprehension questions

Speaking: discussing facts

Reading and speaking: jigsaw reading/information gap, asking and answering questions, group discussion of advantages and disadvantages

Writing: a personal profile

Pronunciation: intonation

Estimated time: 7–8 hours

You're Amar, aren't you? (pages 36–37)

Warm-up

- Tell the class to stand up. Divide them into three groups roughly the same size. One group is the verb *be,* another groups is the verb *do* and the last group is the verb *have.*
- Explain that you're going to say the names of different tenses. If you say, for example, the Present simple, the *do* team have to all sit down quickly because *do* is the auxiliary verb used to make questions and negatives for this tense. Continue the activity with the names of the main tenses in random order, e.g. Past simple, Present perfect, Present continuous, Past continuous, etc.

1

- Refer students to page 36 and to the photo of Lisa and Amar. Ask them where they are and elicit that they are in a supermarket or shopping centre.
- Play the recording. Students listen and read the text.

Transcript  1.32
See Student's Book page 36.

LEARN IT! USE IT! TRANSLATE IT! Ask the students to find the expressions in the text. Check understanding by asking them to give you the equivalent expressions in their language.

2 Comprehension check

- Students read the text again and answer the questions. They check their answers in pairs. Check answers as a class.
- Ask students what they think about the relationship between Lisa and Rob. Elicit any acceptable responses, e.g. it might not be a serious relationship because Lisa doesn't know where Rob is and she hasn't spoken to him.

KEY
1 No, he doesn't know her well.
2 Yes, he is very surprised.
3 She says that they decided not to tell too many people.
4 No, he isn't planning to. He isn't sure if he'll see him.
5 She asks him to ask Rob to call her.
6 She thinks Emily will be jealous.

Extension

Pair work: dialogue practice

Play the recording again and ask students to practise the dialogue in closed pairs. Students swap roles when they have finished. Circulate and help with pronunciation and intonation as necessary. Ask a pair of students to act out the dialogue in front of the class.

Grammar Guide · Question tags

- Remind students about the auxiliary verbs that you used in the *Warm-up.* Elicit that an auxiliary verb is a verb that helps the main verb, especially when making negative and interrogative sentences.
- Draw their attention to the statements and to the question tags at the end of each of them. Ask them if they notice any pattern. Elicit that the question tags are formed with the auxiliary verb. If the main verb in the sentence is affirmative, the question tag is negative, while if the main verb is negative, the question tag is affirmative.
- Point out the use of the modal verbs *will* and *could* in question tags. Explain that with modal verbs, we use the modal verb in the question tag.
- Ask the students why they think we use question tags. Explain that we use them to clarify or check what we have just said. We are asking the other person if we are right or if they agree. Question tags are very common in English and contribute to a naturally flowing conversation.

3 Check!

- Refer students to the sentences and question tags and ask them to match them together.
- When they have finished, they check their answers in pairs. Check answers as a class.

KEY
1 e 2 h 3 g 4 b 5 f 6 c 7 a 8 d

Pronunciation • intonation

Remind students that we use question tags to clarify what we've just said in the main part of the sentence. Point out that often we already know the answer to the question, and we use question tags to show we are interested. We use intonation to show this when we use them.

1 Draw students' attention to the two sentences and allow them a little time to read them. Explain that in the first one we're not sure about the answer while in the second one we are. Play the recording and ask the students if they notice any difference in the intonation of the two question tags. Repeat the sentences yourself if necessary. Elicit that in sentence *a* the intonation rises while in sentence *b* the intonation falls. Students listen again and repeat. Encourage them to exaggerate their intonation a little.

Transcript 1.33
See Student's Book page 37.

2 Allow students time to read the sentences. Explain the task. Students listen and choose a or b. They check their answers in pairs.

Transcript 1.34
See Student's Book page 37.

3 Play the recording for students to check their answers. Pause after each sentence to allow students to repeat.

Transcript 1.35
See Student's Book page 37.

KEY
1 b   2 a   3 a   4 b

Extension

Pair work: It is, isn't it?

Divide students into groups of three. Allocate a different scenario to each group. For example, one group is preparing to go on holiday, packing their bags and checking that everything is ready. Another group could be talking about their city, what they like and don't like about it, etc.

In their groups of three, they have to prepare a dialogue. In their dialogue, they have to use question tags as naturally and as often as possible.

Monitor, helping out as necessary and putting any useful vocabulary on the board. Check they are using the question tags correctly. When they are finished, they act out their dialogues for the class. Have a vote on the best dialogue.

---

4 'EU' is 'European Union', isn't it?

- Write *EU* on the board and ask the class if they know what it means. Elicit that it refers to the European Union.
- Divide students into A/B pairs. Tell them they have two minutes to think of anything they know about in the European Union. After two minutes, stop the students and get feedback from each pair, putting their ideas on the board.

- Refer students to the information about the EU and ask them to read through it to see if their ideas were right.
- Students choose the correct alternative. Tell them not to worry if they're not sure, but encourage them to discuss them with their partner and to make a guess.
- When they are ready, refer students A to page 108 and students B to page 111 and explain that they have the answers for different pieces of information. Refer them to the example and explain that they have to check their answers using question tags.
- Monitor the students as they work, listening out for correct use of question tags. Make sure they are using the right verb and switching from affirmative to negative or negative to affirmative.

KEY
1 European Economic Community   2 1957   3 1973
4 2002   5 2004   6 25   7 Strasbourg, Brussels and Luxembourg   8 five

---

Extension

Pair work: EU countries

Students work in pairs. Set them a time limit of three minutes. In their pairs, they write down as many member countries of the EU as they can on a piece of paper.

Stop the students and ask them to swap their answer sheet with another pair. Go through the countries with the students, putting them on the board so that they get the correct English spelling. Tell them to award 2 points for every correct country, and 1 point if the country is correct but the spelling is wrong. Deduct a point if they list a country that's not (yet) in the EU. The pair with the most points wins.

KEY

Austria, Belgium, Bulgaria, Cyprus, the Czech Republic, Denmark, Estonia, Finland, France, Germany, Greece, Hungary, Ireland, Italy, Latvia, Lithuania, Luxembourg, Malta, the Netherlands, Poland, Portugal, Romania, Slovakia, Slovenia, Spain, Sweden, the United Kingdom

---

5 You know me well, don't you?

- Draw students' attention to the four categories and explain that each student should write one sentence about their partner for each category (two positive and two negative). Tell them not to ask their partner for information, but to guess what they think is true.
- In their pairs, students check the sentences using question tags. Remind them to use rising intonation if they are unsure of the answer and falling intonation if they are sure. Their partner should agree with them and give more information or disagree with them and correct them.
- Monitor the activity, listening out for correct use of structure and intonation. When the activity has finished, ask a few pairs to perform the activity for the whole class.

Homework
Workbook p.18 Ex.2 & p.21 Ex. 10
Key p.100

I found a text which Rob had sent me pages 38–39

Warm-up

- Write the names of the following characters on the board: *Rob, Emily, Lorenzo, Lisa*. Tell the students they have a minute or two to think about how the characters are connected.
- Get feedback from a few pairs. Elicit that Rob and Emily used to be a couple, but they split up when Emily started to like Lorenzo. (This happened in *New Horizons 1*, so students may not remember well.) Now, Lisa likes Rob and she recently told Amar that they're a couple.
- Get brief feedback about what the class thinks of the situation.

6

- Refer students to the photo of Lisa and ask them to think of an adjective to describe how she looks. Possible answers could include confused, worried, upset, sad, unhappy, miserable etc.
- Play the recording. Students listen and read the diary entry.

Transcript 🔊 1.36

See Student's Book page 38.

LEARN IT! USE IT! TRANSLATE IT! Remind the students of these expressions in the dialogue. Check understanding by asking them to give you the equivalent expressions in their language.

7 Comprehension check

- Students read the text again and put the events of the story into the correct order. They check their answers in pairs. Check answers as a class.
- Ask the students why they think Lisa looks miserable or upset in the photo. Elicit that she feels silly for telling Amar that she and Rob were a couple and that she's sad because Rob just wants to be friends.

KEY

a 5   b 4   c 2   d 6   e 1   f 3

Grammar Guide • Past perfect

- Draw students' attention to the structure of the Past perfect. Ask them if it looks a little bit similar to any other tense they know and elicit that it is similar to the Present perfect. Point out that the Past perfect always contains *had* + past participle – there is no different form for the third person singular. Make sure students are clear on the structure of the affirmative, negative and interrogative forms.
- Explain that we use the Past perfect to talk about the past before another past action or time. This means it is often used with the Past simple. It is an efficient way of separating a story into different times without having to explain it.
- Draw their attention to the example and elicit that the actions in the Past perfect happened first, while the actions in the Past simple happened second.
- Highlight the linking words that are commonly used with the tense and check for understanding.

8 Check!

- Students complete the sentences with the correct form of the verbs in brackets. Remind them to think carefully about the order of events: whichever one happened first will be in the Past perfect.
- They check answers in pairs. Check answers as a class.

KEY

1 had just left…rang   2 got…had started
3 didn't feel…had eaten   4 came…had missed
5 had just got…started   6 had finished…realised
7 walked…had left   8 was…had had

Extension

Pair work: By the time I got home, …

Students work in pairs. Tell each student to write five sentences using the Past simple. Tell them they should describe a past action. For example, *I switched on the TV*. Monitor, helping out as necessary.

When they are ready, they swap sentences with their partners. Tell them to use their partner's sentences to make new ones. They should include *after, because, by the time, when* and *just* one time each and should add another event in the past perfect. For example, *I switched on the TV because I had finished my homework*.

Monitor, helping out as necessary. When students have finished, they compare their sentences in their pairs.

---

9 Vocabulary • relationships

- Refer students back to the text on page 38 and ask them to find the words highlighted in bold. Explain that they are all related to relationships.
- Ask the students if they notice anything about the words and elicit that they are phrasal verbs and expressions. Tell them to use the context of the words to guess their meaning and to translate them into their own language.
- Explain that if they need to use a dictionary, they should be careful. For example, if they want to look up *make it up*, they have to check that they have this exact phrase in the dictionary. If they go to *make*, they will see a long list of phrasal verbs and it is important to identify the correct one.
- In pairs, students check their answers. Check answers as a class, putting the correct translations on the board.

KEY

Students' own answers.

Extension

Pair work: relationships

Students work individually and think of a couple that they know. If they don't want to think about a couple they know, or don't know one, they can invent a fictional couple or use a famous couple.

They make some notes about the couple's relationship. Encourage them to use the vocabulary from exercise 9. When they are ready, they work in pairs and tell each other the story of their chosen couple. Monitor, helping out as necessary. Encourage them to use relationship vocabulary and the Past perfect tense when they can.

---

10 Rob had changed

- Refer students to the text and ask them to read through it quickly, ignoring the gaps, to find out how Rob changed after he split up with Emily. Elicit that he started to change his image and that he became more self-confident.

- Students complete the text using the Past perfect form of the verbs in the box. They check their answers in pairs. Check answers as a class.

KEY

1 had liked   2 had been   3 hadn't argued
4 had begun   5 had decided   6 had felt
7 had been   8 had made   9 had realised

11 What had happened?

- Explain to the students that they are going to listen to a conversation between Amar and Jackie. Put the following question on the board: *How many people do they talk about?* Play the recording and students answer the question. They check their answer in pairs. Elicit that Amar and Jackie talk about four people: Gwyneth, Lisa, Emily and Rob.

- Refer students to the questions and allow them time to read them. Remind students to identify key words to help them. When they are ready, play the recording a second time. Students answer the questions. They check their answers in pairs. Check answers as a class.

- Divide students into A/B pairs. Students A tell students B about Jackie's evening. They then swap, and students B tell students A about Amar's evening. Remind them to use the Past perfect and Past simple correctly, depending on the order of events. Monitor, helping out where necessary.

Transcript 🔊 1.37

Jackie Hello?
Amar Hi, Jackie – it's Amar. Did you get back to Cardiff safely after the IYJC meeting yesterday?
Jackie Yes, I did, thanks. I had a really nice evening yesterday.
Amar Really? What happened?
Jackie Well, before I came to London I'd arranged to go to my friend Gwyneth's house when I got back, so she came to meet me at the station. But when we got to her house, all my other friends were there, too! She'd phoned them all and organised a surprise party last night, to celebrate my birthday again now I'm back in Wales!
Amar Oh, how lovely!
Jackie I know! They'd all got there early and decorated the room, and they'd even made me a big cake with 17 candles on it! Then they'd hidden with the lights off until I came in and they jumped out and surprised me! It was great!
Amar That sounds brilliant. I'm glad you managed to celebrate your birthday with all your friends there!
Jackie How about you, what have you been up to?
Amar Nothing much, really. I went to the shopping centre this afternoon to get some paper for my printer, and after I'd bought that I bumped into Lisa.
Jackie Lisa?
Amar She's Emily's friend, who's American. Apparently she's going out with Rob, which is a bit strange because although I knew Emily had told Rob it was over, I thought he still liked her. I didn't know he'd started seeing someone else.

Jackie Well, it's good if he's managed to get over her. Though if I was Lisa, I'm not sure I'd want to go out with someone my friend had been out with!
Amar Yes, that's what I thought. Anyway, after I'd finished talking to Lisa, I went to the library to see if they had a book Rob had told me about. It sounded really interesting, and I think it might be useful for my article for the IYJC.
Jackie Did you manage to get it?
Amar No, someone had already borrowed it. I think I might call Rob tomorrow and see if I can borrow his.
Jackie That's a good idea – and you can find out all the gossip about him and Lisa!

KEY

1 She had arranged to go to her friend Gwyneth's house.
2 She had arranged a surprise birthday party for her.
3 They had decorated the room and made her a big cake, and then they'd hidden with the lights off.
4 He had gone to the shopping centre to get some paper for his printer.
5 He went to the library to borrow a book.
6 Somebody had already borrowed the book he wanted.

Homework

Workbook p.18 Ex.1 & p.19 Ex.3–6
Key p.100

She told me that she was your girlfriend page 40

12

- Draw students' attention to the picture of Amar and Rob at the top of the page. Ask them what they think they are talking about. Elicit that they are probably talking about what Lisa said to Amar in the shopping centre.

- Allow students time to read the sentences. Play the recording. Students decide if they are true or false and check their answers in pairs. Play the recording a second time to check answers as a class. Students correct the false sentences.

Transcript 🔊 1.38

Amar Hi, Rob. This is Amar.
Rob Hi, Amar. How are you?
Amar I'm fine thanks. I was just wondering if I could borrow that book you told me about last week? I think it might be useful for my article for the IYJC. Would it be OK if I came over to get it later?
Rob Yes, of course. I'll be in all afternoon, and you can keep it as long as you like.
Amar Thanks, Rob. Hey, by the way, I saw Lisa at the shopping centre. I didn't know about you and her! That's great! She seems nice.
Rob What do you mean?
Amar Well, she said you were going out together. She told me that she was your girlfriend.
Rob What? That's not true! We've only been out together once. What else did she say?
Amar Well, she said you had decided not to tell too many people, because you wanted to keep it quiet. How strange!
Rob We went out once last week, that's all. I decided after that I didn't want to go out with her. She's not my girlfriend!
Amar She also said you didn't want Emily to know. She said Emily would probably be jealous.

Rob I can't see why. Emily finished with me. We're just friends now so I don't see why she would be interested if I liked someone else. But honestly – Emily told me she couldn't stand Lisa and now I'm beginning to see why!

Amar Well, Lisa was looking for you. She said she hadn't seen you yesterday but that she had phoned you that morning.

Rob Yes… she left me a message about the date we were supposed to have last night.

Amar So did you go out with her last night?

Rob No, I didn't. I sent her a text yesterday afternoon and cancelled the date. I told her I just wanted to be friends and that I didn't want to go out with her again.

Amar Hmm… well, I'm sorry if I embarrassed you. But I think Lisa's probably more embarrassed right now!

KEY
1 T.
2 F: He says they've only been out together once.
3 F: He says he can't see why Emily would be jealous.
4 T.
5 T.
6 F: He says he cancelled the date.

Grammar Guide • Reported speech • *say, tell*

- Draw students' attention to the column on the left and point out that the statements are direct speech. We know they're direct speech because of the quotation marks around them. Refer them to the column on the right and explain that this is reported speech. Reported speech is when we tell another person what somebody else said. The most common reporting verbs are *say* and *tell*.

- Explain that we have to change three things when we move from direct speech to reported speech. (1) We have to change the pronouns so that they are logically correct. For example, *Rob said 'I don't like Lisa'* becomes *Rob said that he didn't like Lisa. I* becomes *he.* (2) We have to move one tense back to the past. In the previous example, the Present simple *don't like* becomes Past simple *didn't like.* Point out how each tense changes to a specific tense. (3) We have to change any references to time. For example, '*Rob said 'I went to bed early last night'* becomes *Rob said that he had gone to bed early the night before. Last night* becomes *the night before*, because we are reporting what Rob said at a different time.

- Including *that* after *say* is not absolutely necessary, but it is quite common.

> **LOOK OUT!** Students often have difficulty distinguishing between *say* and *tell*. Grammatically, the difference is that we must include an object after *tell* but never after *say*. We *say something* but we *tell someone something*. *Tell* implies that we are giving someone direct information, while *say* is more general.

13 Check!

- Students complete the reported speech sentences using the correct tenses or words. Encourage them to refer to the *Grammar Guide* to make sure they are using the right tense.

- Students check their answers in pairs. Check answers as a class.

KEY
1 was meeting   2 could   3 had never smoked
4 would see…the next day   5 had seen…the night before   6 was

14 She said…

- Tell the students they are going to listen to a description of a famous actor. Encourage them to make any notes they can as they listen.

- Play the recording the first time. Ask students to compare their notes in pairs. Play the recording a second time. They compare their notes again to complete them.

Transcript 1.39

I'm a really big fan of … I've liked him ever since I was a child. He was born into a middle-class family in West Philadelphia in the USA in 1968. He started off as a DJ under the name The Fresh Prince with his friend Jeff Townes. His first acting role was on a TV sitcom *The Fresh Prince of Bel-Air* in 1990. His first film was *Six Degrees of Separation*. His first really successful film was *Bad Boys*, and then he was in *Independence Day*. He had enormous success with his film about Muhammad Ali called *Ali* and then as the policeman in *I, Robot*. He's working on a new film at the moment. He's become one of the richest and most successful black actors in the history of the cinema. I think people will remember him as one of the truly great stars. Oh, and he's very sexy too!

KEY
Students' own answers.

15

- Using their notes, students make sentences reporting what the speaker said. Monitor, helping out as necessary. When they are ready, they compare their sentences. Monitor, listening carefully to their use of tenses and check that they are changing pronouns and time references correctly.

- Students try to guess who the actor is. Play the recording for them to check their answer.

Transcript 1.40

I'm a really big fan of Will Smith. I've liked him ever since I was a child. He was born into a middle-class family…

KEY
Will Smith.

ALREADY FINISHED? Students think of five things that people said to them today and make reported speech sentences. The activity can be set for homework.

Homework
Workbook p.20 Ex.7–9
Key p.100

Grammar Check page 41

Question tags

1
1 are   2 was   3 didn't   4 have   5 won't   6 couldn't

2
1 affirmative   2 negative

Past perfect

3

1 Past perfect   2 past participle

4

2 It had stopped snowing by the time we got off the bus.
3 He went to hospital because he had fallen off a ladder.
4 He didn't feel thirsty when he had drunk some water.
5 He went to live in Spain after he had left university.

5

Affirmative: you'd, it'd, had
Negative: hadn't
Interrogative: Had, Had
Short answers affirmative: had, had
Short answers negative: hadn't, hadn't

Reported speech • *say, tell*

6

Past simple, Past continuous, Past perfect, Past perfect, *would*, *could*

7

1 c   2 a   3 b

8

1 She told me she was going to the party.
2 ✓
3 I said that he couldn't borrow my bike.
4 You told him you weren't very happy.
5 He told her that I was ill.

9

1 He told me he wanted to go to the library the next day.
2 She said she was studying Chemistry at university the following year.
3 He said he'd do the shopping that afternoon.
4 You told us he couldn't come to the party the following week.
5 They said they had gone to the beach that day.
6 They told me they had just been to an exhibition.

| Homework
Workbook p.21 Revision
Key p.101

Skills and culture   pages 42–43

Warm-up

• Write *love* on the board and tell students to work in pairs. Ask them to discuss whether they believe in love at first sight (falling in love when you first see somebody) or not.

• After a minute or two, get some feedback from a few pairs. Encourage them to explain their answers.

1 Listening

• Draw students' attention to the photo and ask them what they see. Elicit that it is a photo of an elderly couple.

• Explain that Emily is interviewing the couple. Play the recording. Students find out where Eric and Joan met. Check the answer as a class.

• Refer students to the questions and allow them time to read through them. Play the recording a second time.

They answer the questions and check their answers in pairs. Check answers as a class.

Transcript 1.41

Emily You've been married for a very long time, haven't you, Joan?
Joan Yes, we have… nearly 60 years.
Emily 60 years! That is a long time.
Eric Yes, but we're still happy. Even after all these years.
Emily That's great! Now tell me, how did you meet?
Joan Well, it was very different from now. There weren't any dating agencies or anything.
Eric No. We met at work. Well, I was working in a shop, a greengrocer's, and Joan used to come in with her mother to get fruit and vegetables.
Joan Yes, that's right. The first time I saw him I really liked him. He was so cheerful and friendly. And he never got angry, even though there were some difficult customers.
Emily And what did your mother think of Eric?
Joan Oh, she didn't have any idea that I liked him. But I remember her telling Eric's boss one day what a nice, polite young man Eric was!
Emily So when did you ask her out, Eric?
Eric Well, I had to wait quite a long time, because she always came in with her mother. I kept hoping she'd come in on her own one day. Then one day she did, and I asked her out.
Emily And where did you go on your first date?
Eric I collected her from her house and we went for a coffee and after that we went to the cinema.
Emily And when did you get serious?
Joan Oh, very soon. After about two months he asked me to marry him. I was a bit surprised. He was my first boyfriend, you see.
Emily And when did you get married?
Eric We got married about six months after that first date.
Emily That was very quick, Eric.
Eric I suppose it was, but I didn't want to lose her, you see. And it was the best decision of my life!
Joan Oh, Eric!

KEY

Eric and Joan met in a greengrocer's.
1 They've been married nearly 60 years.
2 She used to go with her mother to get fruit and vegetables.
3 She said he was a nice, polite young man.
4 He was waiting for her to come into the shop on her own.
5 They went for a coffee and then they went to the cinema.
6 They got married about six months after their first date.

2 Speaking

• Remind the students that Joan said there hadn't been any dating agencies when she met Eric. Ask them if they know what a dating agency is and elicit any ideas from the class.

• Refer students to the four types of dating mentioned, and explain that they are different ways of meeting people for possible relationships. In their pairs, students discuss what they know about them.

• Monitor, helping out with ideas or vocabulary as necessary. Get some feedback from each pair. Put good suggestions on the board for the whole class to see.

Students' own answers.

> **CULTURE NOTE** **Speed dating** happens at an organised event. It is a way of meeting a large number of people in a short period of time. People usually have a time limit of a few minutes to ask each other a few questions. Then, if they like somebody, they can follow it up. **Text dating** refers to relationships that begin by communicating through text messages. **Internet dating** is when people have a profile on the Internet for other people to see. If they like somebody, they can contact them and arrange to meet. **Dating agencies** are businesses that specialise in matching two people together.

3 Reading

- Divide students into A/B pairs. Refer students A to text A and students B to text B. They skim-read their texts and identify which method of dating their character tried.
- Check answers as a class.

KEY
Ant: speed dating
Louise: text dating

4

- Remind students that in longer texts they will usually come across words that they do not understand. Sometimes it is okay to ignore these words, as they may not be important for understanding the whole text, but other times it is essential to know them.
- If it is essential to know them, they should work out the meaning from the context. If they have time, they can check the word in a dictionary. Remind them that if they are in an exam situation, they will not have time and they may not have a dictionary so it's good to practise working out the meaning from the context.
- Students read their respective texts and identify six words they do not know that they think are necessary to understand. They apply the above steps: guessing from the context and then checking in a dictionary.
- Monitor, helping out as necessary.

KEY
Students' own answers.

5 Reading and speaking

- Students work in their A/B pairs. Refer them to their relevant questions and ask them to interview each other about their texts.
- Monitor, helping out as necessary. Check answers as a class.

KEY
Louise
1 She tried to meet people through text dating.
2 It's very easy to do.
3 It might be dangerous because you don't know who's sending you a message.
4 She didn't have anything in common with them and they had lied to her.
5 She realised she had wasted her time with text dating.

Ant
1 He tried to meet people through speed dating.
2 The event was held in a trendy bar.
3 He spoke to each person for three minutes.
4 He spoke to about 15 people in total.
5 He didn't get on very well with them.

6

- Remind students of the four types of dating they saw in exercise 2. Refer them to page 108 and allow them time to read through the definitions of each type. Monitor, helping out as necessary. Encourage them to add any other types of dating that they know about.
- Put students into groups of three or four. In their groups, they discuss the advantages and disadvantages of each type of dating and rank them in order of preference. Encourage them to explain why they chose their ranking.
- Monitor, helping out with vocabulary or ideas as necessary. When students have finished, join groups together so that they can compare their lists. Do they agree or disagree with each other?

7 Writing

- Refer students to Louise's profile and allow them time to read it. Ask them if they would like to meet her. Get some feedback from a few students, encouraging them to explain their answers.
- Students write a similar profile for themselves. Tell them to follow the structure that Louise uses. Remind them to check their writing for any grammar or spelling mistakes. The activity can be set for homework.

Extension
Language plus p.92

Language review pages 44–45

Vocabulary

1

1 went   2 got   3 put   4 cheated   5 split   6 lied
7 love   8 fell   9 engaged   10 getting

2

Transcript 1.42

See Student's Book page 44 and Key.

3

1 upset   2 embarrassed   3 relieved   4 annoyed
5 worried   6 confident   7 bored   8 jealous

Grammar

4

Possible answers:
1 upset/annoyed/jealous   2 relieved   3 confident
4 bored/annoyed   5 jealous   6 annoyed/upset
7 worried   8 embarrassed

5

1 S   2 S   3 F   4 S   5 F   6 F   7 S   8 F

6

Students' own answers.

7

1 aren't you   2 do they   3 hasn't she   4 do they
5 don't we   6 can he   7 did she   8 couldn't you
9 isn't it   10 isn't he

8

Possible answers:
2 …they liked living in a city.
3 …she didn't have curly hair.
4 …they lived with their parents.
5 …we didn't have to tidy our room every week.
6 …he could ski.
7 …didn't lose my mobile.
8 …could get a good job.
9 …it wasn't/weren't really cold today.
10 …wasn't/weren't using the computer.

9

Students' own answers.

10

1 I phoned Jackie when I had finished my homework.
2 We walked home because we had missed the bus.
3 He had fallen asleep by the time the film finished.
4 My parents went home after they had talked to the teacher.
5 I stopped playing football because I had broken my ankle.
6 She changed her image after she had moved to Paris.

11

Jane told me (that) Owen was a nice person.
Jane told me (that) he couldn't dance.
Jane told me (that) they had enjoyed their meal together.
Jane told me (that) she would go out with him again.
Owen said (that) he liked Jane a lot.

Owen said (that) she was going to teach him to dance.
Owen said (that) he was going to invite her to a concert.

Communication

12

1 make   2 up   3 well   4 keep   5 a   6 couldn't
7 What   8 into

Extra Practice
CD-ROM

Topic and vocabulary

Crime and punishment

Requests

Addictions

Mistakes in life

Grammar

should have, ought to have

Reported speech • *ask, tell, want*

Functions

Talking about past mistakes

Reporting questions

Reporting requests and instructions

Skills and culture/pronunciation

Speaking: discussing opinions, reflecting on the article

Reading: predicting content, comprehension questions

Listening: true or false

Writing: a story

Pronunciation: silent consonants

Estimated time: 7–8 hours

You should have called the police pages 46–47

Warm-up

- Write *crime* on the board and divide the class into pairs. Explain that they have two minutes to brainstorm as many types of crime as they can.
- After two minutes, stop the students. Get feedback from each pair, putting their suggestions on the board.

1

- Refer students to page 46 and to the photo of Sophie and Amar. Ask them where they are and elicit that it looks like they're in a library or bookshop.
- Play the recording. Students listen and read the text.

Transcript ⊙ 1.43

See Student's Book page 46.

LEARN IT! USE IT! TRANSLATE IT! Ask the students to find the expressions in the text. Check understanding by asking them to give you the equivalent expressions in their language.

2 Comprehension check

- Students read the text again and answer the questions. They check their answers in pairs. Check answers as a class.
- Write *brave* and *cowardly* on the board and ask students which of these adjectives would describe Sophie best.

Elicit that she is brave because she shouted at the mugger.

KEY

1 No, she isn't.
2 She was working as an intern on the biggest newspaper in Toronto.
3 She saw a mugging the previous night.
4 He thinks she could have got hurt.
5 Nothing. He ran away without the wallet.
6 No, he was just bruised and shaken up.

Grammar Guide • *should have, ought to have*

- Draw students' attention to the sentence *You shouldn't have done that* in the text. Ask the class what Amar is talking about and elicit that he is talking about what Sophie did (she yelled at the mugger). Explain that Amar is giving Sophie advice about something that happened in the past. In other words, Sophie cannot change what she did, but Amar is telling her his opinion about it.
- Write this sentence on the board: *Sophie yelled at the mugger.* Ask the students how we form past advice and elicit that we use *should + have* + past participle, and we switch from positive to negative and negative to positive. Therefore we can say *Sophie shouldn't have yelled at the mugger.*
- Point out that *ought to* can be used in the same way as *should,* although it is not very common to use it in negative or interrogatives except in very formal situations.

3 Check!

- Refer students to the incomplete sentences and ask them to complete them together.
- When they have finished, they check their answers in pairs. Check answers as a class.

KEY

1 should   2 ought   3 shouldn't   4 should   5 ought

Extension

Pair work: They should have done it differently…

Ask students if they have seen the film *Titanic*. Elicit some information about the film and the key events in the story from the class. As a class, ask them to think of what the people in charge of the ship should have done differently or what they shouldn't have done. Get some ideas at random, encouraging students to use *should/shouldn't have* and *ought to have* in their sentences.

Ask the class to work in pairs and to think of another important event in history. It can be international or it can be specific to their country, but it should be something about which we can give past advice. Help out with ideas as necessary.

Each pair writes five sentences saying what should have been done differently. Monitor, making sure they are forming their sentences correctly. When they have finished, get some feedback from each pair.

---

4 Vocabulary • crime and punishment

- Remind students of the crimes they brainstormed at the beginning of the lesson and refer them to the vocabulary in the box. Ask them to tick the words that they thought of.
- Explain the chart below the vocabulary box, pointing out the different columns. In pairs, students arrange the words into their categories. Encourage them to work with the words they already know before doing new vocabulary.
- Check answers as a class. Ask students to translate each word for homework.

KEY

nouns:
crimes: drug-dealing, shoplifting, vandalism, joyriding, mugging
criminals: pickpocket, drug dealer, burglar, shoplifter, thief
verbs:
crimes: beat up, vandalise, break into, steal, burgle, mug, attack
police: investigate, question

Extension

Pair work: types of stealing

Write the following crimes on the board: *shoplifting, burglary, theft, robbery, mugging.* Ask students what they all have in common and elicit that they are all related to stealing.

In their pairs, students decide what the difference is between each of the crimes. They may use their dictionaries if necessary. Monitor, helping out where it is needed.

Get feedback from each pair about the differences between them. Which of them do they think is the most serious?

KEY

Shoplifting is when people take things from a shop without paying.
Burglary is when somebody breaks into somebody else's house and takes things from it.
Theft is a general word for stealing something secretly.
Robbery is associated with taking money from a bank or post office.
Mugging happens on streets and can be quite violent.

---

5 I shouldn't have done that

- Draw students' attention to the six pictures. Allow them some time to look at them and get some brief feedback about each picture by asking the students what they see in them.
- Explain the task. In pairs, students discuss what they think happened in each picture. Monitor, helping out as necessary. Encourage the students to use the vocabulary they learned in exercise 4.
- When they are ready, students write their own sentences about each picture using *should* or *shouldn't*. They compare their sentences in pairs. Get some feedback from each pair.
- Explain that the class will hear six people describing what happened in each picture. Students match each speaker

with a picture. Check answers as a class. Were their original guesses right?

Transcript 🔊 1.44

1 I went to work but I forgot to close the window. While I was out, someone burgled my house. They stole my DVD player and my stereo.
2 I went shopping and I had my mobile in my back pocket. When I got home, it wasn't there. I think a pickpocket took it. I lost all my friends' numbers – how annoying!
3 I left the keys in my car when I went into a café to get a coffee. When I came back, it had been stolen. I'll never do that again!
4 I took a short cut home across the park in the dark. Suddenly a mugger grabbed me and made me give him all the money I had with me. It was really terrifying. You should never walk through a park on your own at night.
5 I left my MP3 player on the front seat of my dad's car while we went into town for lunch with my uncle. Someone broke into the car and stole the MP3 player. It took me ages to save up for a new one!
6 I bought a new car and a few weeks later I had to park it in a bad area of town at night. When I came back it had been vandalised. Someone had broken the windows and scratched the paint with a key. I couldn't believe it!

KEY
1 E   2 C   3 B   4 A   5 F   6 D

6 I should have done my homework

- Tell students about something your parents used to complain about when you were at school. For example, *When I was at school, my parents used to complain about me staying up late. They used to say 'You should have gone to bed earlier last night! That's why you're tired after school!'*
- Working individually, students think about three things that their parents complain about. Point out that they can create complaints if they want to. They should use *should/ ought to have* or *shouldn't have* to write their sentences. Monitor, helping out with vocabulary as necessary.
- When they are ready, they compare their sentences with a partner. Get some feedback from each pair.

ALREADY FINISHED? Students think of complaints that they would like to hear from their parents. Refer them to the example. Encourage them to be creative in their sentences.

Homework
Workbook pp.24–25 Ex.1–4
Key p.101

She asked if she could see my article! pages 48–49

Warm-up

- Write the following questions on the board: *Did you finish your homework? Have you tidied your room? Do you fancy going to the cinema at the weekend?*
- Ask the class who would be the most likely people to ask these questions and accept any suggestions.

7

- Refer students to the photo of Emily and Amar and discuss it briefly with them. Elicit that they are standing beside a river or canal and that there is a bridge in the background. Point out the boats to the students and explain that they are called punts. (See the Culture note below.)
- Play the recording. Students listen and read the dialogue.

Transcript 🔵 1.45

See Student's Book page 48.

> **CULTURE NOTE** Punts are small flat-bottomed boats (see photo) that are used in shallow water such as canals or small rivers. A pole is used to move the punt along by pushing it against the bottom of the river. Punts are common in Oxford and Cambridge, for example.

LEARN IT! USE IT! TRANSLATE IT! Remind the students of these expressions in the dialogue. Check understanding by asking them to give you the equivalent expressions in their language.

8 Comprehension check

- Students read the text again and tick the questions that Sophie asked Amar. Check answers as a class.
- Ask the students why they think Amar and Emily think about Sophie. Elicit that they don't know her very well yet but that they do not trust her very much.

KEY

Sophie asked Amar questions 1, 4, 5, 6 and 8.

Grammar Guide • Reported speech • *ask*

- Draw students' attention to questions 1 and 4 in exercise 8. Ask them what the answer to question 1 must be and elicit that it must be a place because of the question word *where*. Ask them what the answer to question 4 is and elicit that it will either be *yes* or *no*. Point out that question 1 is an open question (there are many possible answers) and that question 4 is a closed question (the answer can be *yes* or *no*).
- Ask students to find questions 1 and 4 in the dialogue in exercise 7. Elicit that with all reported questions we go back one tense in the past, as well as making the necessary changes to pronouns and time references (see the discussion of reported speech on Student's Book page 40). With *yes/no* questions we have to use *if*, while with open questions we use the question word again.
- Go through the examples with the class, making sure they understand the structure of reported speech with *ask*.

9 Check!

- Students reorder the words to make questions. Explain that they then have to use the pronouns in brackets to make reporting questions. Refer them to the example.
- They check answers in pairs. Check answers as a class.

KEY

2 Are you going to see him again? She asked me if I was going to see him again.
3 Have you seen the film? I asked her if she had seen the film.

4 Where are you working? They asked me where I was working.
5 What did you do yesterday evening? He asked them what they had done the evening before.
6 Are you English? We asked her if she was English.
7 Who is your favourite singer? She asked me who my favourite singer was.
8 Is Mark from the USA? I asked him if Mark was from the USA.

Extension

Pair work: She asked me if…

Put the following categories on the board: *food, music, holidays, plans for the weekend, last weekend, family, best friend, film*. Ask the students to work individually to make a question for each of these categories. For example, *How often do you eat chocolate?* or *What is your favourite food?* It doesn't matter what the question is as long as it is related to the category. Monitor, helping out as necessary.

When they are ready, they work in pairs and ask and answer each other's question. Encourage them to make a note of their partner's answers.

When they have finished, divide the class into new pairs. Each student tells each other about the questions they asked their previous partner and how they answered. For example, *I asked Siobhan what her favourite food was and she told me it was pizza.* Monitor, paying attention to the students' use of reporting questions.

Pronunciation • silent consonants

Explain that many common words have silent consonants that we do not pronounce. While the spelling includes these consonants, we need to know when to pronounce them.

1 Students listen to the recording and repeat. Repeat the words yourself. Encourage the class to copy you. Elicit that we do not pronounce the *k* in *know* or the *h* in *when*.

Transcript 🔵 1.46

See Student's Book page 49.

2 Students work in pairs and underline the silent consonants. Play the recording for them to check their answers. Students listen again and repeat.

Transcript 🔵 1.47

See Student's Book page 49 and key.

KEY

1 w   2 gh   3 l   4 l   5 h   6 t   7 gh   8 l   9 l   10 k
11 w   12 t

10 She asked her if…

- Refer students to the photo and ask them who they see. Elicit that Rebecca and Sophie are in the photo. Students listen and read the dialogue.
- Tell students to close their books and to try to remember the conversation between Rebecca and Sophie. In pairs, they use reporting questions to describe the conversation.
- Monitor, helping out where necessary and checking for correct use of reporting sentences. Get some feedback from each pair about the dialogue.

Transcript 🔊 1.48

See Student's Book page 49.

Extension

Pair work: dialogue practice

Play the recording again and ask students to practise the dialogue in closed pairs. Students swap roles when they have finished. Circulate and help with pronunciation and intonation as necessary. Ask a pair of students to act out the dialogue in front of the class.

---

11 Speed dating!

- Ask the class if they can remember what speed dating is. If they can't, refer them to pages 42 and 43 of the Student's Book to refresh their memories.

- Explain to the class that they are going to have a speed dating event. Each student has to write down three questions that they would like to ask to find out about somebody. Monitor, helping out with ideas or vocabulary as necessary.

- When students have finished their questions, divide them into small groups. They ask and answer each other's questions. Circulate, making a note of any errors you might like to come back to later.

- When students have finished, they report the most interesting questions that were asked of them to the rest of the class. Remind them to use reporting questions as they speak. Check for correct use of reporting questions.

Homework
Workbook pp.25–26 Ex.5–6
Key p.101

He told me to ring you (page 50)

12

- Draw students' attention to the picture of Emily and Steve. Ask them how they look and elicit that they look worried.

- Play the recording and ask students to identify who they are talking about. Elicit that they are talking about Sophie.

- Draw their attention to the sentences and allow them some time to read through them. When they are ready, they listen to the recording a second time and identify who says the sentences. They check answers in pairs. Check as a class.

Transcript 🔊 1.49

Emily Hello, Steve?
Steve Hi, Emily! What's the problem? You sound worried.
Emily Yes, I am. I saw Amar and he told me to ring you. Have you heard?
Steve What?
Emily About the last finalist in the competition.
Steve No. Who is it?
Emily It's a Canadian girl called Sophie MacDonald. She's just arrived in London.
Steve Right. Look, calm down. What's the problem?
Emily Well, Amar and Rebecca have both met her and apparently she's a brilliant journalist.
Steve Oh… How do they know?

Emily Well, Rebecca says she's won loads of competitions before and Amar says she's writing an amazing article about street crime in Britain. She's been working as an intern for the *Toronto Times* and they wanted her to stay on!
Steve That's a bit worrying. But what's she like?
Emily Well, she's a bit nosy. She asked Amar to show her his article.
Steve And what did he say?
Emily He told her she couldn't see it.
Steve Good for him.
Emily And she wanted him to tell her about all the other competitors.
Steve But why?
Emily I don't know. But I think she's really determined to win the competition.
Steve Well, we can't do much about it, can we? We'll just have to do our best.
Emily I suppose so, but I'm really worried all the same.
Steve Yeah, it doesn't sound good.
Emily Amar asked me to find out more about what she's written.
Steve That's a good idea. But how?
Emily He told me to find out about the *Toronto Times*. Apparently she wrote loads of articles for them so maybe we could see what they're like.
Steve Well, I'm near the library – I'll go and see if they have any copies of the *Toronto Times*.
Emily OK, Steve. You do that and I'll look on the Internet to see what I can find.
Steve OK, Emily. Good idea. I'll see you back at home later.

KEY
1 E **2** S **3** E **4** E **5** E **6** S **7** S **8** E

LANGUAGE TIP Point out the pattern that follows *ask, tell* and *want* when we are giving orders or making requests. Go through the examples and make sure students understand the structures.

LOOK OUT! Emphasise the difference between the use of *ask* in making questions for information and requests. With questions for information we use the normal method of reporting the questions. With requests, we use the infinitive (see *Language Tip*).

---

13 *ask, tell, want*

- Students use the prompts to make reporting sentences using the words in brackets.

- Students check their answers in pairs. Check answers as a class.

KEY

1 Steve asked Emily what Sophie was like. / Steve asked Emily if she could tell him what Sophie was like. / Steve asked Emily to tell him what Sophie was like.
2 Steve told Emily to calm down.
3 Emily wanted Steve to find out more about her.
4 Sophie told Amar to tell her about his article.
5 Emily asked Steve to go to the library. / Emily asked Steve if he could go to the library.
6 Amar didn't want Sophie to read his article.
7 Steve asked Emily what Amar had said.
8 Emily asked Steve if he had heard about Sophie.

Extension

Pair work: When I was younger, my parents…

Tell students to think about things that their parents told them to do when they were younger. For example, go to bed early, tidy their room, etc. Ask them to think of five things.

When they are ready, they work in pairs and tell each other what their parents told them to do. Monitor, listening for correct use of *ask, tell* or *want*. Get some feedback from each pair.

14 What did he ask him to do?

- Ask the class how well they can remember the story of the competitors for the IYJC so far and elicit some answers. Refer students to the four statements and ask them to try to identify which one is false, without looking back through the book.
- Students check their answers in pairs. They check the dialogues to see if they were correct.

 KEY

1 is false.

15

- Ask the students to write three sentences using *want, tell* and *ask* about the story so far. Explain that they can look through different dialogues and base their sentences on any part of the story they like. They should include one false statement.
- Monitor, helping out as necessary and making sure that students are forming the sentences correctly.
- When they are ready, they compare their sentences and identify which one of their partner's sentences is false.

Homework

Workbook pp.26–27 Ex.7–10
Key pp.101–102

Grammar Check   page 51

should have, ought to have

1

1 c   2 a   3 b   4 d

2

1 She should have gone to the dentist.
2 They shouldn't have travelled to London by car.
3 I ought to have brought a book with me.
4 She shouldn't have spent all her money.
5 You should have told me you were late.
6 They shouldn't have stayed at that hotel.

Reported speech • ask

3

1 liked   2 was   3 had eaten…the night before
4 could   5 had done…before   6 was going   7 was
8 had got

4

1 the same as   2 if   3 don't use

5

1 Robert asked me if I was going to the club that evening.
2 I asked Rachel if she liked pizza.
3 Anna asked me where I got off the bus.
4 Aidan asked Kate if she was in the school basketball team.
5 She asked me what I had done at the weekend.
6 I asked Jane when she was going on holiday.

Reported speech • ask, tell, want

6

1 O   2 R   3 O
Students' own translations.

7

1 I told them to turn down the TV.
2 He wanted me to help him with his Geography homework.
3 I asked her to tidy her bedroom.
4 They wanted me to work late that evening.
5 She told me not to park my scooter in front of her house.
6 Martin wanted me to play squash with him later that day.
7 I asked them if they wanted a cup of coffee.
8 The teacher told her to finish her homework.

Homework

Workbook p.27 Revision
Key p.102

Skills and culture   pages 52–53

Warm-up

- Students work in pairs. Tell them they have one minute to think of things that are illegal to do in their country.
- When they are ready, get some feedback from each pair.

1 Speaking

- This exercise can be very sensitive. If you don't feel it is appropriate for your group, you can skip it completely.
- Draw students' attention to the list of drugs and allow them time to read through them. If you like, you could ask the students to do some research on these drugs for homework, so that they find out more about them. The activity can then be completed in a later class.
- In pairs, they tick which drugs are legal to use in their countries. Direct the discussion towards the issue of legal drugs like alcohol, caffeine and tobacco and elicit their harmful effects on health. Get some feedback from each pair.
- In their pairs, they discuss each drug and decide whether they should be legal or not. Encourage them to expand their answers as much as possible by giving reasons or examples to support their opinions.
- Monitor, helping out as necessary. To round the activity off, bring the discussion to the whole class.

Extension

Pair or group work, whole class: addictions

As an alternative to exercise 1, you can do a different lead-in activity. Write the following on the board: *shopping, computer games, alcohol, illegal drugs, medicine, gambling, smoking, coffee.*

Elicit or pre-teach the meaning of any unfamiliar vocabulary.

Ask students to discuss the following questions:

Which addictions do you think are the most serious? Put them in order of seriousness. What makes you think so?

Which addictions do you think are the most difficult to give up? What do you think can help?

2 Reading

- Refer students to the two photos and ask them to compare them. Point out that they are photos of the same person, but at different times.
- Refer them to the questions and allow them a little time to discuss them in their pairs. Get some feedback from each pair.

KEY
Students' own answers.

3

- Refer students to the text. Ask them to skim-read to find out if they were right about Lucy. Remind them that a skim-read means reading quickly in order to get a general understanding of what a text is about.
- After about two minutes, stop the students and ask them for some feedback.

4

- Ask students to read the questions. Point out that they should try to identify key words that will help them locate the answers in the text.
- Students answer the questions and check their answers in pairs. Check answers as a class.

KEY
1 Lucy started getting bullied at school.
2 They stopped giving her pocket money.
3 The teenagers are asked to do schoolwork as well as jobs around the ranch.
4 They have rules about appearance to stop the teenagers from hiding behind their cool mask. This helps them look inside at what is confusing them and what is causing their problematic behaviour.
5 Lucy has started a college course, she's got a part-time job and she volunteers to help underprivileged children.
6 She wants to try to achieve something with her life.

5

- Draw students' attention to the words in bold in the text. Remind them that instead of using a dictionary, it is quicker and more effective to use the context of an unknown word to work out its meaning.

- Students match the words to their synonyms or definitions. They check their answers in pairs. Check answers as a class.

KEY
1 take responsibility 2 misbehave 3 underprivileged
4 shoplifting 5 well-being 6 disciplined 7 attitude
8 problem behaviour

6 Speaking

- Refer students to the questions and allow them time to read them. Encourage them to take a few minutes to make a note of any ideas or interesting points that they would like to mention.
- Divide the students into small groups. They discuss the questions. Encourage them to develop their answers as much as possible and to respond to each other's opinions.
- Monitor, helping out with vocabulary or ideas as necessary. Put any new vocabulary that arises on the board for the whole class to see.
- When students have finished, get some feedback from each group about each question. Finish off the activity by having a brief class discussion on the questions.

KEY
Students' own answers.

7 Listening

- Refer students to the *Study Strategy* in the Student's Book and read it with them. Explain that they are going to listen to an interview with the manager of a drug rehabilitation centre.
- Ask students to read the sentences and to follow the instruction they read about in the strategy. Encourage them to underline key words to help them focus as they listen. Explain that they will hear the recording twice, so that if they do not get the answers during the first listening, they should not worry because they will hear it a second time.
- Play the recording. Students check their answers in pairs. Play the recording a second time. Check answers as a class.

STUDY STRATEGY Read the instructions with the students. Point out that they should maximise the time before they listen to try to predict what the recording is going to be about. They can do this by reading the questions and the task carefully. It's useful to know that the questions follow the order of the recording. In this way, they not only know what to listen for, but they can also focus on the recording.

Transcript ◉ 1.50

Woman How long have you been working here, Jim?
Jim Er, I came to the centre about, er, two years ago.
Woman And how many residents do you have?
Jim We have space for fifteen people. At the moment we've got nine residents and we're interviewing another person this afternoon.
Woman What exactly do you do here?
Jim We offer a residential programme for drug addicts. We try to discover why they use drugs so we can help them to stop.

Woman I see. And how do you help them?

Jim Er, we try to teach them different strategies for dealing with, er, those problems, without using drugs.

Woman What are the problems facing a heroin addict who wants to stop?

Jim Well, it depends, but for many addicts the biggest problem is finding somewhere safe and supportive for them to stay while they're dealing with the problem, so they don't get involved with their old drug-taking environment and friends again.

Woman What percentage of people manage to stop using heroin?

Jim Er, it's difficult to say. But the longer people stay with us the more likely they are to stop using drugs.

Woman So how long does the average treatment last?

Jim We offer a residential programme lasting twelve months.

Woman And how many people work here?

Jim We've got a staff team of six.

Woman Finally, what advice would you give to people who are curious to try drugs?

Jim Well, I would tell them to think carefully about their life now – their friends, their family, their possessions, their hobbies.

Woman Why?

Jim Because the people I work with here, the people who have decided to use drugs, well, they've lost everything – their family, their friends, their home and their possessions – sometimes even their liberty. If you don't want to lose them, don't take drugs.

KEY

1 F: There are nine clients in the centre at the moment.
2 T.
3 T.
4 F: The longer people stay, the more likely they are to stop using drugs.
5 F: The programme lasts for twelve months.
6 T.

8 Writing

- Read the instructions with the class and make sure they know what they have to do. In their pairs, they invent the story, following the prompts.

- Monitor the students as they work, helping out with ideas or vocabulary where necessary.

- When they are ready, students write their stories based on the notes they have made. This activity can be set for homework.

- Have a class feedback session on the students' stories. Each student presents their story to the rest of the class. The other students take notes and vote for the best story in the class.

Extension
Language plus p.94

Exam plus 5

Objectives

To practise exams related to the material covered in Unit 5

Use of English: Word formation

Writing: Semi-formal email

Speaking: Situational role-play

Use of English • Word formation page 54

Warm-up

- Ask the class if they can think of any crimes that are new. Allow them about two minutes to discuss ideas in pairs.
- When they are ready, get suggestions from each pair and put them on the board. Do any of the students know anyone who has been a victim of any of these crimes?

1

- Write *cybercrime* on the board. Ask the class to look at the word to tell you what it means. Elicit that it means crime that is committed using information technology, especially crimes that occur on the Internet.
- Read the instructions carefully with the class and check that they understand exactly what they have to do.
- Ask the students what they think 'word formation' means. Elicit that it means changing the form of one word to make a different type of word. We can change words from verbs to become nouns, or adjectives to become adverbs and so on.
- Look at the first gap with the students. Ask them what kind of word they need to complete the gap and elicit that they need a verb. Ask the students to go through the rest of the gaps and to identify what kind of word they need in each case. Check answers as a class.
- Refer students back to the first gap and ask them to change the form of the verb *be* so that it grammatically fits into the sentence. Elicit that the correct answer is *been*.
- Students complete the task by themselves. Point out that there may be places where the form of the word does not need to be changed.
- They check their answers in pairs. Check answers as a class.

KEY

1. been (verb: present perfect)
2. easier (comparative adjective)
3. have (verb: present perfect)
4. examples (plural noun)
5. extremely (adverb)
6. advertisement (noun)
7. pretend (verb: base form)
8. shopping (verb: -*ing* form)
9. illegal (negative adjective)
10. careful (adverb)

> **EXAM TIP** Point out that the first thing to do in this type of task is to identify what kind of word is needed in each gap. This makes it easier to change the form of the word.

Writing • Semi-formal email page 54

2

- Read the instructions carefully with the class and make sure they understand what they have to do. Point out the four pieces of information they have to include.
- Ask the class what the features of a semi-formal email are, and elicit that a semi-formal email will contain an informal structure but will contain slightly more formal language. The language should not be as informal as it would be in an email to a close friend.
- Before they write, tell students to think about the four pieces of information they have to include and to make some notes about what they are going to say. This will help them to stay on track as they write and will prevent them from forgetting anything. Point out that it is not enough to simply list the different points in their emails, but that they will need to connect it together so that it flows naturally.
- Students write their emails. Allow them about 15–20 minutes to write it, depending on the strength of the class. Alternatively, students can do it for homework and bring the letter to the next class for correction.
- Remind them to read their emails when they have finished to check for mistakes and that they have included all of the information asked of them.

> **EXAM TIP** Point out the importance of making sure they check their writing for the basic requirements asked of them.

Speaking • Situational role-play page 110

3

- Read the instructions with the class and make sure they understand what they have to do. Tell students to turn to page 110 and draw their attention to the four proposals. Check their comprehension, and pre-teach any unfamiliar vocabulary – or allow the use of dictionaries for the preparation stage.
- Divide the class into groups. Explain that they need to look at all four proposals and discuss them in their group in order to decide which of them they think is best. Encourage them to make notes on the advantages and disadvantages of each proposal.
- Monitor the groups as best you can, making sure that they are discussing each proposal properly. Make a note of any errors you feel you would like to address later, but don't interrupt the students as they speak.

4

- Divide the class into new groups. Ideally, each new group will consist of students who were in different groups for the first stage of the activity.
- Each student presents their views to their new group. Encourage the group to discuss and to reach an agreement on which proposal is best.
- Monitor, helping out as necessary but without interrupting the students too much.
- When students have finished, get some feedback from each group.

Encourage students to make notes during the first stage of the activity. This will help them summarise what they discussed in their first group instead of going through the whole discussion for a second time.

Functions bank
Workbook p.51

Further exam practice
Workbook p.32–33

Exam plus 6

Objectives

To practise exams related to the material covered in Unit 6

Reading: True / False / Not stated

Listening: Multiple matching

Speaking: Picture-based discussion

Reading • True / False / Not stated page 55

Warm-up

- Ask the students what they like about their country and if they are proud to be from their country. In pairs, they have two or three minutes to discuss. Encourage them to give reasons for their ideas.

- Get some feedback from each pair. Do the rest of the students agree?

1

- Ask the class what they should call somebody who comes from the UK. Elicit any answers and put them on the board.

- Ask the class to skim-read the text to find out what the correct answer is. Elicit that there is no correct answer and that it depends on how each person views their nationality and identity.

- Read the instructions for the task with the students and draw their attention to statements 1–8. Make sure students understand the task fully.

- Tell the students that as they now have a general idea of the text from their skim-read, they can start to do the task. Allow them time to read through the statements and ask them to underline key words that will help them locate the answer in the text.

- When students are ready, do the first statement together as an example. Ask the students which part of the text this information should be in and elicit that it should be at the beginning of the text in the first paragraph. Ask them if the text says that this is true and elicit that it doesn't. Ask them if it says the information is false and elicit that it does not. The students should be able to tell you that this information is not in the text and therefore the correct answer is N.

- Students continue with the remaining statements. Ask them to underline the relevant parts of the text where they can find the answers. They check their answers in pairs. Check answers as a class.

KEY
1 N 2 T 3 T 4 F 5 F 6 T

It's important that the students understand the difference between True, False and Not stated. T and F can only be chosen if there is evidence in the text that directly supports or contradicts the statement. They must otherwise choose N.

Listening • Multiple matching page 55

Warm-up

- Ask the students to work in pairs. They have two or three minutes to discuss what kind of voluntary work they would like to do. For example, what kind of charity would they support and what kind of work would they be willing to do.
- When they are finished, get some feedback from each pair.

2

- Read the instructions with the class. Explain that there will be six speakers and that they can each be matched to one of the statements A–H. Point out that there is an extra statement the students will not need.
- Emphasise that it is important to maximise the time before a listening exercise as much as possible and that students should read the statements carefully. This will help them predict the kind of things they should listen for.
- Allow students time to read the statements, encouraging them to underline key words. Check for understanding.
- Do the first one together as a class as an example. Play the recording until the // symbol. Stop the recording and ask the students to tell you what they heard. Elicit some feedback and then ask them to match the speaker to the best statement. Elicit that the best statement for speaker 1 is C.
- Play the recording from the beginning again. Students do the task and check their answers in pairs. Play the recording a second time. Check answers as a class. If you feel it is necessary, play the recording a third time, pausing after each speaker so that the students understand why the answers are correct.

Transcript 🔊 2.02

1 I've been volunteering for a local environmental charity for almost five months now. I usually do it at the weekends and I help raise awareness of climate change and global warming by handing out leaflets in the street. I think it's very important to volunteer for something that you care about. //

2 Well, I don't have much free time to volunteer, as I'm too busy with my schoolwork. And anyway, if I had time to work, I'd rather get a part-time job in a restaurant or a shop. The way I see it, you should earn money if you're going to work – not do it for free!

3 I volunteer twice a week at a home for the elderly. I enjoy it, although sometimes it can be difficult to combine with my studies. I usually just go there to keep the people company and chat to them. Some of them have amazing stories about the past so it can be very interesting. I think it's very worthwhile and it makes a big difference to their days.

4 When I'm older, I want to be a vet. I love animals! But it will be difficult, and I'll have to study very hard to get a place at university. That's why I volunteer at a local centre for homeless dogs. The experience will make a real difference in my future career so I don't mind that I'm not making any money.

5 I definitely think that volunteering is a good idea. I don't have the time to do it, however, as I spend all of my free time playing sports. My older sister volunteered abroad last year. She spent a month in a small village helping the local people start a school. She had an amazing experience there!

6 When I finish school, I want to go travelling for a year. I'm not sure where I'll go, but I want to see as much of the world as possible. I also want to do something useful while I'm away, like help people who are not as well off as here in the UK. I think that everybody has a responsibility to do something to help others.

KEY

1 C   2 F   3 A   4 H   5 D   6 B

> **EXAM TIP** When students underline key words, they should be aware that they may not necessarily hear that word in the recording. Instead, they should listen for synonyms or for phrases that mean similar things. For this reason, it is important for the students to build their vocabulary as much as possible.

Speaking • Picture-based discussion page 55

3

- Draw students' attention to the three pictures at the bottom of the page. Ask them what they can see and elicit a brief description of each photo from the class.
- Read the instructions with the class and read through the prompts with them. Make sure they understand what they have to do.
- Explain that they are going to use the photos along with the prompts to have a discussion about raising money for charity. Emphasise that although the prompts are in question form, they should not simply be answered directly but should help to generate ideas that can support the discussion. Point out that they should try to speak about each of the ideas mentioned in the prompts.
- Divide students into small groups of three or four and tell them to start the task. Don't worry if students don't start speaking immediately, as they may take a little time to organise their ideas.
- Monitor the students as they discuss. Try to make sure that the discussion in each group is balanced and that students are not only speaking, but also allowing other students time to give their opinion. Make a note of any general errors students make, and observe how they link their ideas together. Try not to interrupt the students in their discussion.
- When students have finished, get some feedback from each group about the main ideas they discussed. If you like, and if the students are able, you could bring the discussion to a class level for a few minutes to round off the activity.

Functions bank
Workbook p.51

Further exam practice
Workbook p.32–33

Topic and vocabulary

Charities and world problems

The news

Soccer Aid

Raising money for charity

Grammar

Past simple passive

Present perfect passive

Present continuous passive

Future passive

Reflexive and reciprocal pronouns

Functions

Talking about past facts

Talking about developments

Skills and culture/pronunciation

Speaking: discussing facts, situational role-play

Reading: reading for gist, general comprehension

Listening: true or false

Writing: semi-formal letter

Pronunciation: homophones

Estimated time: 7–8 hours

It's time this abuse was stopped (pages 56–57)

Warm-up

- Write *charity* on the board. Ask students if they know what it means and elicit that a charity is an organisation that tries to help people who are in need, e.g. homeless people, refugees, etc.
- Have a quick brainstorm with the class and ask them to give you the names of any charity organisations that they know. Put their suggestions on the board. Ask them to briefly describe what the charity they mention does.

1

- Draw students' attention to the text and explain that Rob is a volunteer with Amnesty International. Ask the students to look at the logo for the organisation in the top left-hand corner of the text and to think about what it means. Elicit that the logo consists of a candle and barbed wire. The wire symbolises oppression, while the candle symbolises hope.
- If students haven't already mentioned the organisation, ask them if they can guess from the logo what Amnesty International does. Elicit that it is a charity which tries to help people whose human rights are not respected.
- Students listen and read the text.

Transcript 2.03

See Student's Book page 56.

LEARN IT! USE IT! TRANSLATE IT! Ask the students to find the expressions in the text. Check understanding by asking them to give you the equivalent expressions in their language.

2 Comprehension check

- Students read the text again and answer the questions. They check their answers in pairs. Check answers as a class.

KEY

1 It is a movement of ordinary people from across the world that stands up for human rights.
2 Arms trading.
3 More than one million people.
4 It launched a campaign to ask governments to sign an International Arms Trade Treaty.
5 He swam there to hand in a petition in support of the campaign.
6 He raised £3,780.

Extension

Individual work: meaning from context

- Ask students to look back through the text to find and underline six words that they do not know. Using the context of the words, encourage them to guess their meaning. They can check their ideas in a dictionary.

Grammar Guide • Past simple passive, Present perfect passive

- Ask students to tell you how the passive is constructed (covered in *New Horizons 3* Unit 8). Elicit that we use *be* + past participle. Ask them to give you any example of the passive in the Present simple and elicit any answers, e.g. *Coffee is produced in Brazil.*
- Point out that we can use the passive form in other tenses as well. Draw students' attention to the Past simple passive forms and go through the examples with them. Ask them what is different about it and elicit that the verb *be* is in the Past simple form. Otherwise, it is structured the same way as the Present simple and it follows the same rules.
- Draw their attention to the Present perfect form and elicit that the verb *be* is now used in the Present perfect.
- Make sure students understand the structure of the affirmative, negative and interrogative forms.

3 Check!

- Refer students to the sentences and ask them if they are active or passive. Elicit that they are active. Explain the task. Students change the sentences to the passive form.
- When they have finished, they check their answers in pairs. Check answers as a class.

KEY

1 The agreement was signed by the G8 countries.
2 The World Cup in 2010 was won by Spain.
3 The exam has been marked by two different teachers.
4 *The Tempest* was written by Shakespeare.
5 The building was painted last year.
6 The letters haven't been typed by his secretary.

4 What was published?

- Refer students to the incomplete sentences and explain the task. Remind them to think about which tense is more suitable in each case: Past simple (for finished actions at a specific past time) or Present perfect (for actions at an unspecific past time which still have an effect on the present).

- Play the recording for the students to check their answers. For each situation, ask them to write down some extra information. Get brief feedback on which of the facts the students find most surprising.

- Working individually, students write five sentences of their own. Ask them to think about their family and to try to use examples of both tenses in their sentences. Point out that two of the sentences should be false.

- Monitor, helping out with ideas and vocabulary as necessary. Check that students are forming their sentences correctly.

- When they are ready, they compare their sentences in pairs and try to identify the false sentences. Get some feedback from each pair.

Transcript 🔊 2.04

1 A dog was sent into space in 1957. Her name was Laika and she was in the Russian spaceship *Sputnik 2*.

2 A long time ago, tea was used as money in Siberia. It was their currency until the nineteenth century.

3 The first phone book was published in New Haven, Connecticut. The book only had one page, with fifty names on it.

4 No diamond bigger than 3,106 carats has been found. The mammoth Cullinan diamond was discovered in February 1905 in South Africa.

5 Albert Einstein was asked to be the President of Israel in 1952. He said no.

6 In the USA, more people were killed by dogs in the year 2002 than have been killed by Great White sharks in the last 100 years. So perhaps we should be more scared of Scooby Doo than of Jaws!

KEY

1 was sent   2 was used   3 was published   4 has been found   5 was asked   6 have been killed

Extension

Pair work: America was discovered in…

Students work in pairs. Tell them they are going to make a short history quiz with five questions. If necessary, allow them to research their questions for homework. Each question should be in the passive (Past simple or Present continuous). For example, *When was America discovered?*

Monitor the students as they make their questions. When they are ready, they join another pair. Each pair asks each other the questions. The other pair should answer with a full sentence using the correct passive tense. For example, *America was discovered in 1492.* Point out that it doesn't matter whether they get the answers right and that they should guess.

Monitor the activity, listening out for correct use of the passive. When students have finished, get some feedback. Which team got all of the questions right?

5 Vocabulary • charities and world problems

- Draw students' attention to the words in the box and explain that they are all related to charities and different kinds of world problems.

- Ask students to look through them and to tick the words that they already know. When they are ready, they compare the words they know with their partner, explaining to each other any that the other does not know.

- Point out that the first letter of each word is given in the incomplete sentences. Students do the task and check their answers in pairs. Check answers as a class.

- Ask students to guess the meanings of the words they do not know from the context of their sentences. Get feedback from the class to make sure they have the right understanding.

KEY

1 famine…disease…poverty   2 raise money… orphanage…starve   3 Volunteers…collection… homeless   4 telethon…donate   5 Aid…crisis   6 petition…refugees   7 human rights   8 sponsor… charity

Extension

Group work: charity work

Students work in small groups. Ask them to discuss the different problems in exercise 5 and to decide which one of them is the most serious. When they have decided, they should think of what kind of charity they could set up to fight the problem. What events would they have? What would they call it?

Monitor the students as they discuss. Make sure they are using the vocabulary correctly and make a note of any errors you want to come back to at a later time.

ALREADY FINISHED? Students think of problems in the world and write three sentences about them, leaving a gap to be filled by one of the words from exercise 5. Their partner guesses the words.

Homework
Workbook pp.28–29 Ex.1–3 & p.30 Ex. 7
Key pp.102–103

Who will be chosen as the winner? pages 58–59

Warm-up

- Remind students about the IYJC competition and elicit the names of the competitors. Tell them to refer to page 4 of the book to refresh their memories if necessary.

- In pairs, ask them to decide who they think is going to win the competition. After one or two minutes, get some feedback from the class.

6

- Draw students' attention to the photo and ask them who they see. Elicit that Rebecca and Jackie are in the photo. Ask them where Jackie comes from and elicit that she comes from Wales.

- Play the recording. Students listen and read the dialogue.

Transcript ⊙ 2.05

See Student's Book page 58.

LEARN IT! USE IT! TRANSLATE IT!   Remind the students of these expressions in the dialogue. Check understanding by asking them to give you the equivalent expressions in their language.

7 Comprehension check

- Students read the text again and decide if the sentences are true or false. They check their answers in pairs. Check answers as a class.

- Ask the students who Rebecca wants to win the competition. Elicit that she doesn't mind as long as it isn't Sophie.

KEY

1 F: The winner will be announced at the prize-giving ceremony.
2 T.
3 T.
4 F: The prize will be a six-month contract with a newspaper.
5 F: She doesn't have a clue who will win.
6 T.

Extension

Pair work: dialogue practice

Play the recording again and ask students to practise the dialogue in closed pairs. Students swap roles when they have finished. Circulate and help with pronunciation and intonation as necessary. Ask a pair of students to act out the dialogue in front of the class.

Grammar Guide • Present continuous passive, Future passive

- Remind students of the structure of the passive form.

- Ask them what the Present continuous form of the verb *be* looks like and elicit *am/is/are being*. Go through the examples with the class, and make sure they understand the structure of the Present continuous passive.

- Refer them to the examples of the Future simple passive and check for understanding of the structures. Remind students that they are used just like the other passive forms they have seen and that they are just in different tenses.

8 Check!

- Students put the words into the correct order to make sentences.

- They check answers in pairs. Check answers as a class.

KEY

1 The car won't be repaired by tomorrow.
2 The TV programme is being interrupted.
3 The wedding dress will be finished in time.
4 The painting is being restored by an expert.
5 What time will the gates be opened?
6 I'm afraid it won't be done until Thursday.

7 Are you being taught by Mr Cooper?
8 Julia will be given a scooter for her birthday.
9 Are the Taiwanese students being met at the airport?
10 We aren't being asked for our opinion.
11 Will your article be published in a newspaper?
12 The garden isn't being looked after.

9 The news is being broadcast

- Explain to the students that they are going to listen to a news bulletin. Don't point out the exercise in the book just yet and ask them to prepare to make notes in their exercise books. Point out that when they make notes, they don't need to write down full sentences and that they just need to write down the main points that summarise what they hear.

- Play the recording. Ask students to compare their notes in pairs and to complement each other's where necessary.

- Refer them to the incomplete text and to the vocabulary in the box. They use their notes to complete the text in the correct passive form. Remind them that they may need any form of the passive so they just look carefully at the sentence to think about which tense they need.

- They check their answers in pairs. Play the recording a second time to check answers as a class.

Transcript ⊙ 2.06

See Student's Book page 59 and Key.

KEY

1 has been seen   2 are being made   3 is being hit
4 has been damaged   5 will be repaired   6 is expected
7 are being taken   8 are being asked   9 will be done
10 is being tested   11 will be presented   12 has been rescued   13 will be treated

Extension

Pair work: Did you hear the news?

Students work in pairs. Ask them to discuss the news items they just listened to in exercise 9. They should report what they heard to each other and then decide which of the news items was most interesting or surprising.

Monitor the activity, listening out for correct use of the passive tenses as the students speak. Get some feedback from each pair.

10 Your own news bulletin

- Tell the students to imagine that they are journalists. They have to create two stories each. Refer them to the suggested topics, or ask them to think of their own topic if they like.

- Remind them that they should be using the passive where possible. Monitor as they work, helping out with ideas and vocabulary where necessary.

- When they are ready, students work in pairs and combine their stories so that they have a news bulletin with four items. Ask them to plan the order of their stories. When they are ready, they present their news to the class.

- Encourage the other students to make notes as they listen. When all of the news bulletins are finished, have a class vote on which pair had the most interesting stories and on which pair would make the best newsreaders.

ALREADY FINISHED? Students make questions about their own stories for the rest of the class to answer. Encourage them to make about one question per story. Monitor the activity to make sure the questions are correctly formed and are logical.

Homework
Workbook p.29 Ex.4–6 & p.30 Ex.12
Key pp.102–103

I don't want to go by myself! page 60

11

- Draw students' attention to the photo and ask them how the three girls look. Elicit that it looks like they're happy and that they're having fun. Ask them what they think they're talking about and elicit any acceptable answers.
- Play the recording. Students listen and find out who the three people are that they are talking about.
- Refer students to the sentence halves and ask them to read through them. Explain that they have to match them together as they listen again, so they should underline key words that will help them identify their answers.
- Play the recording a second time. Students check their answers in pairs. Check answers as a class.

Transcript 2.07

Jackie So what do you know about this Canadian girl? Is she really as amazing as everyone's saying?

Emily You mean Sophie. Yes… Amar's a bit worried. He said she had a fantastic idea for the competition. And she's not only a brilliant journalist but she's stunning too, apparently! Ugh.

Rebecca But when I was talking to her I got the impression she's a bit full of herself.

Jackie Well, I'll be stunning too for the final. I'm going to buy myself a new dress to wear. I saw a fantastic red dress at a shop round the corner from here.

Rebecca I brought a dress with me from New Zealand, but I think I'll treat myself to a new pair of shoes.

Emily I still haven't got a clue what I'm going to wear. The only thing I know is that I don't want to go to the ceremony by myself! I think I might invite Rob, otherwise he won't be able to come.

Rebecca Come on! You're not inviting him just to be nice to him. Tell the truth! You're hoping you'll start going out with each other again!

Emily I don't know… But I feel much better when he's around and I think he's changed a lot lately. He didn't use to be very sure of himself, but he seems a lot more confident now. Perhaps we could try again… But keep it to yourselves – I know he's your cousin, but don't tell him, Rebecca!

Rebecca I won't say a word, don't worry!

Jackie Anyway, let's promise we'll try and enjoy ourselves, whatever happens!

KEY
They talk about Sophie, Amar and Rob.
1 d 2 e 3 a 4 c 5 b

LEARN IT! USE IT! TRANSLATE IT! Remind the students of these expressions in the dialogue. Check understanding by asking them to give you the equivalent expressions in their language.

> **LANGUAGE TIP** Draw students' attention to the reflexive pronouns. Explain that we use them when we do an action to ourselves. For example, *I'm making myself a cup of coffee.* or *They've bought themselves a new house.* Point out that the reflexive pronouns must always match with the subject of the sentence.
>
> Reflexive pronouns can be used to emphasise who does an action. For example, *She didn't get any help with the painting. She painted it herself.*
>
> Reciprocal pronouns are used to talk about how two or more people direct the same actions at themselves. For example, *The twins John and Dermot argue with each other every day* or *When we got to the party, Chris and Joanna were dancing with each other.*

12 Reflexive or reciprocal?

- Draw students' attention to the verbs in the box and to the incomplete sentences. Explain that they need one of the verbs along with a reflexive or reciprocal pronoun to complete each sentence logically.
- Students do the task and check their answers in pairs. Check answers as a class.

KEY
1 hurt myself   2 killed herself   3 enjoy yourself
4 love each other   5 blame yourself
6 introduced themselves   7 known each other
8 greeted each other   9 like each other
10 promised myself

Pronunciation · homophones

Write *sun* and *son* on the board. Ask the class to say each word and if they notice anything about them. Elicit that they have different spelling and different meanings but that they are pronounced in the same way.

Ask them how they know which word is meant if they hear one of them. Elicit that it is usually easy to know which word somebody's using from the context.

1 Students listen to the recording and repeat. Repeat the words yourself. Encourage the class to copy you.

Transcript 2.08
See Student's Book page 60.

2 Students find words on page 56 that have the same pronunciation but different spellings to the words in exercise 1. Check answers as a class.

KEY
1 check 2 their 3 new 4 peace 5 to 6 rights

Homework
Workbook p.30 Ex.8–11
Key p.103

Grammar Check page 61

Past simple passive, Present perfect passive

1

1 *Ulysses* was written by James Joyce.
2 Ice has been discovered on Mars.
3 Mr and Mrs Madison weren't invited.
4 Your car hasn't been damaged.
5 Was the party organised by the school?
6 Have the students been informed?

2

1 has been burgled 2 was written 3 haven't been invited 4 was taught 5 were…allowed 6 haven't been bullied

Present continuous passive, Future passive

3

a Future passive
b Present continuous passive

4

1 It won't be finished tomorrow.
2 Dinner is being cooked by my brother.
3 Will you be met at the airport by Harry?
4 Is the road being repaired this month?
5 The course will be completed by the students by October.

5

1 A skyscraper is being built in my town.
2 A review will be written when the film comes out.
3 Beethoven's *Fifth Symphony* will be performed next week.
4 A lot of invitations have been sent.
5 ✓

Reflexive or reciprocal pronouns

6

Students' own translations.

7

1 - 2 each other 3 herself 4 each other 5 -
6 himself

Homework
Workbook p.31 Revision
Key p.103

Skills and culture pages 62–63

Warm-up

• Ask the students to work in pairs to discuss what they think would be the best way to raise a lot of money quickly for charity. Allow them about two minutes to decide.

• Get some feedback from each pair. Which is the best suggestion in the class?

1 Speaking

• Draw students' attention to the logos of the famous charities and ask them if they recognise any of them. Get some feedback from the class if any.

• Refer students to the multiple-choice questions. Ask them to guess what they think is the correct answer in each case. When they are ready, they work in pairs and compare what they have chosen. Encourage them to explain why they chose their answers to each other.

• Monitor, helping out as necessary. When the students have finished, refer them to page 111 and ask them to check their answers. Get some feedback about what they think for each of the facts.

KEY
See Students' Book page 111.

> **CULTURE NOTE** **UNICEF** is an international organisation. It is part of the United Nations and it is a shortened form for the United Nations Children's Fund. It provides food and healthcare to children who need it all around the world. The **Terrence Higgins Trust** is a British charity that tries to raise awareness on issues related to HIV and AIDS. It is named after one of the first British people who died from AIDS in 1982. The **WWF** is an international organisation that works on issues related to the environment, wildlife and nature. It supports around 1,300 environmental and conservation projects worldwide.

2 Reading

• Draw students' attention to the photos of the celebrities on page 63. In pairs, they briefly discuss if they know them.

• Get feedback from the class.

KEY
Photo on left: Robbie Williams, a famous English pop singer.
Photo on top right: Diego Maradona, a famous Argentinean football player.
Photo on bottom right: Pierluigi Collina, a famous Italian football referee.

3

• Refer students to the title and ask them what they think the text is going to be about. Elicit that it will probably be about an event that raises money by using soccer.

• Ask students to skim-read the text to check their ideas. After no more than two minutes, stop the students and ask them what Soccer Aid is about.

KEY
Soccer Aid is a charity event that raises money for UNICEF.

> **LANGUAGE NOTE** **Soccer** is the American English term for 'association football' – the game known in the majority of the world simply as 'football'. They use the word to distinguish it from the sport the world calls 'American football' but which the Americans refer to as 'football' or sometimes 'gridiron football'. In American football, players are allowed to pick up the egg-shaped ball, run with it and throw it. Other popular football games around the world include two different types of rugby (Rugby Union and Rugby League – played to different rules), Australian rules (or 'Aussie rules') football, and Gaelic football, which is played in Ireland.

4

- Students read the questions. Remind them that, having done a skim-read, they should be able to target the relevant part of the text in which they can find their answer.
- Students answer the questions and check their answers in pairs. Check answers as a class.

KEY

1 There are more than 166,000 main charities in the UK.
2 The captains were the TV chef Gordon Ramsey for the Rest of the World and Robbie Williams for England.
3 The match was refereed by the Italian referee Pierluigi Collina.
4 England beat the Rest of the World 2-1.
5 It has made over £2.5 million.
6 The money will be used to help children in poor countries.

5

- Draw students' attention to the words in bold in the text. Remind them that instead of using a dictionary, it is quicker and more effective to use the context of an unknown word to work out its meaning.
- Students translate the words into their own language. Check the translations as a class or ask the students to check their translations in a dictionary.

KEY

Students' own translations.

6 Listening

- Tell the class they are going to listen to Gemma talking about what she has done for charity. Refer students to the photo of Gemma and to the picture of the charity logo. Ask them what kind of charity she volunteers for and elicit that it is a charity for children with serious illnesses.
- Refer students to the sentences and allow them some time to read them. Point out that they should read the sentences carefully and identify key words that will focus them on their answers.
- Play the recording and students do the task. They check their answers in pairs. Play the recording a second time. Check answers as a class

Transcript ⊚ 2.09

Gemma Last year we found out that my cousin was suffering from leukaemia. He's only nine and he's been in a lot of pain and he's also had to have chemotherapy, but he's been so brave. He's still got a great sense of humour and doesn't feel sorry for himself – he's amazing. Anyway, his family were given a lot of support by a charity called the Rainbow Trust Children's Charity, which really helps families with children with diseases like leukaemia. My brother and I decided we really wanted to do something to raise money for them. We asked our friends to help and together we came up with the idea of walking around our town in our pyjamas.

We raised £420 in sponsorship from our friends and family before the event and then one Saturday we all walked around the town in our pyjamas and slippers, carrying baskets to collect money. We walked six miles around the town and we were given another £230 by people who donated their change.

After that we didn't want to stop. We decided to organise some charity events at school, too. We talked to our teachers and arranged a slave auction, which raised loads of money! Teachers were 'bought' by groups of students and had to do everything they said for two hours! The teachers were made to do really funny things, like cleaning the students' football boots, and two of them were asked to dance with each other in the playground – it was brilliant! We've also been holding a cake sale every Friday at school – we make cakes at home and bring them in and sell them at break time, and all the money that has been made goes to the Rainbow Trust Children's Charity.

We've raised lots of money for charity so we really feel like we've done something good, but we've had loads of fun, too. Everyone should try it – it's great!

KEY

1 F: Gemma's cousin has got leukaemia.
2 T.
3 F: They raised £420 before the event and then another £230 during it.
4 F: Students bought teachers at a slave auction.
5 F: They sell cakes every Friday at school.
6 T.

7 Speaking

- Divide students into pairs. Read the instructions and questions with the class and check that they understand what they have to do.
- Encourage them to think of a charity that they think does a good job and that deals with issues that they care about. Remind them to think about the ideas they suggested at the beginning of the lesson for raising money.
- Students do the task. Encourage them to make notes as they plan their event. Monitor, helping out with ideas and vocabulary as necessary.
- When students have finished, each pair presents its charity event to the rest of the class. Have a vote on which event the class thinks will be most successful.

8 Writing

- Divide students into pairs. Read the instructions with the class and check that they understand what they have to do.
- Ask them to think about which celebrity they would like to contact and encourage them to refer to the notes that they made in exercise 7.
- Remind students to plan their letters. This will keep them focused on the task and will help them in case they forget to include something. Point out that they should leave some time at the end to check their writing for any mistakes they may have made.
- This activity can be set for homework.

Extension
Language plus p.96

Language review pages 64–65

Vocabulary

1
Across
4 sponsor 7 refugees 8 donate
Down
1 raise 2 crisis 5 rights 6 starving

2
1 Drug-dealing 2 shoplifter 3 vandalism 4 mugger
5 burglar 6 joyriding

3
Criminal:
1 drug-dealer 2 shoplifter 3 vandal 4 mugger
5 burglar 6 joyrider
Crime:
1 drug-dealing 2 shoplifting 3 vandalism
4 mugging 5 burglary 6 joyriding

Grammar

4

Transcript 🔊 2.10
See Student's Book page 64.
Students' own answers.

5
1 was completed 2 will be announced
3 have been rescued 4 is being repaired
5 were invited 6 has been used 7 were told
8 was asked

6

Transcript 🔊 2.11
See Student's Book page 65.
1 how much they charged
2 the campsite closed
3 them to close at midnight
4 would be locked
5 facitities there were
6 me there was a shop
7 us to bring a form of ID
8 we had passports

7

Transcript 🔊 2.12
See Key in exercise 6.

8
1 yourselves 2 each other 3 himself 4 myself
5 each other 6 themselves

Communication

9
Students' own answers.

10
Students' own answers.

11
1 come 2 of 3 What 4 up 5 Keep 6 Fingers
7 dead 8 can't

Extra Practice
CD-ROM

UNIT 7

Every time I pick up the phone... pages 66–67

Warm-up

- Ask the students what a *diary* is and elicit that it is a journal in which people can keep a record of their appointments. It can also be a place for people to record their thoughts and feelings about different things, and to write themselves a summary of the events of the day.
- In pairs, students briefly discuss whether they think diaries are a good idea or not. Encourage them to think of reasons to explain their answers.
- Ask them to say (if they are willing to share this) if they have diaries, and what sort of thing they record in them.
- Get some feedback from a few pairs.

1

- Draw students' attention to the photos at the top of the page and ask them what is happening. Elicit that Emily is thinking about Rob. Refer them to the handwritten text and elicit that it looks like a diary entry. Ask the class what they think Emily is writing about (without reading the text) and elicit any suggestions they have.
- Students read and listen to Emily's diary entry.

Transcript ◉ 2.13

See Student's Book page 66.

LEARN IT! USE IT! TRANSLATE IT! Ask the students to find the expressions in the text. Check understanding by asking them to give you the equivalent expressions in their language.

2 Comprehension check

- Students read the text again and decide if the statements are true or false. Check answers as a class.
- Ask the class to think of some adjectives to describe how Emily generally feels. Put their ideas on the board, explaining any new vocabulary. For example, *lonely, nostalgic, regretful, foolish*, etc.

KEY

1 F: She is having a hard time finishing the article.
2 T.
3 F: They get along really well now.
4 T.
5 F: She has completely forgotten about him.
6 F: She would like to go out with him again.

3 Vocabulary • phrasal verbs

- Ask students to look at the verbs in bold in the text and to tell you what they notice about them. Elicit that all of the verbs have a particle (a preposition or an adverb) with them. Ask them if they know what these verbs are called and elicit that they are phrasal verbs. (We encountered some other examples of phrasal verbs in Unit 4.)
- Explain that phrasal verbs are very common, especially in spoken or informal English.
- Point out that, depending on the particle and the context, the meaning of the phrasal verb can change. It is therefore a good idea to keep a record of them so that they can remember them.
- Draw students' attention to the definitions and ask them to use the context of the sentences to match them to the phrasal verbs. They do the task and check their answers in pairs. Check as a class.

KEY

1 pick up   2 get on with   3 look forward to
4 wake up   5 go back to   6 grown up   7 put up with
8 break up with   9 fall for   10 get over
11 going out with

Grammar Guide • Phrasal verbs

- Refer students to the four different types of phrasal verbs. Type 1 phrasal verbs do not take any object while Type 2 phrasal verbs need an object. Type 3 phrasal verbs need an object. In this type, the object can come between the verb and the particle or it can come after the particle. Type 4 phrasal verbs have two particles (and adverb and a preposition).
- Refer students back to exercise 3 and point out that all of the phrasal verbs are one of these four types. Remind them that when they come across phrasal verbs, they should look at its structure to decide what type it is so that they can use it correctly.

4 Check!

- Students complete the sentences with the correct form of the phrasal verbs. Remind them to think of the meaning of the verb they need before they decide which one to use.
- They check answers in pairs. Check answers as a class.

KEY

1 picked up 2 get over 3 falling for 4 put up with
5 looking forward to 6 wakes up 7 went back to
8 has grown up

5 Vocabulary • phrasal verbs

- Explain to the class that it is sometimes possible to guess the meaning of a phrasal verb by thinking about the meaning of the particle. For example, *get up* can mean either *stand up* or *wake up*.
- However, not all phrasal verbs can be guessed in this way and we need to use the context to help us.
- Students match the phrasal verbs to the definitions. Encourage them to match the ones they already know or can guess before they think about the more difficult ones.
- They check answers in pairs. Check answers as a class.

KEY

1 g 2 e 3 a 4 h 5 c 6 b 7 d 8 f

6 Mime it!

- Mime a simple everyday activity for the class. For example, mime brushing your teeth and ask the class to tell you what you are doing. Explain that acting without making any noise is called miming.
- Divide students into A/B pairs and explain the task. Allow students A some time to choose which verbs they are going to mime and to think about how they are going to mime them.
- When they are ready they mime five verbs for student B, who has to say what student A is doing. Monitor, helping out where necessary. Encourage students B to say full sentences instead of just saying the verb, e.g. *You're getting up in the morning.*
- When students A have completed their five verbs, they swap roles.

7 Phrasal verb test

- If you like, students can work in the same pairs as in the previous exercise, or you may want to switch them around.
- Read the instructions with the class and make sure they understand the task. They do the activity.
- Monitor, checking that students are forming their sentences correctly. Make sure that, if they are using any

Type 3 phrasal verbs, they are separating the verb and particle if it is necessary.

- Get some feedback from each pair by asking them to read out a couple of their sentences to the rest of the class.

Pronunciation • *r*

Write the letter *r* on the board. Ask the students to say the letter in English. If necessary, say it for them yourself so that they can copy you.

Explain that *r* is not always pronounced in English, especially in British English (it is not incorrect if it is always pronounced, as American English and many regions around the world always pronounce the *r*).

If your own accent is closer to one of the variants pronouncing *r*, you may want to skip this Pronunciation focus to avoid confusing your students.

1 Students listen to the recording and repeat. Repeat the words yourself. Encourage the class to copy you. Make sure they can hear the difference between the two words and that they are able to copy them.

Transcript 2.14

See Student's Book page 67.

2 Students work in pairs and look through the list of words. Encourage them to say them aloud to each other and to decide if they should pronounce the *r* or not. Play the recording to check their answers. They listen and repeat.

Transcript 2.15

See Student's Book page 67.

KEY

1 S 2 S 3 P 4 P 5 P 6 S 7 P 8 S

Extension

Individual writing/class activity: journal of a celebrity

Tell students to think of a celebrity they know about. Ask them to write a diary entry for that celebrity. Point out that they don't have to choose a real celebrity and that they don't have to use real events in the diary. They should use phrasal verbs and relationship vocabulary as they write.

Monitor the students as they write. Help out where necessary and check they are using the vocabulary correctly.

When students have finished, collect the diary entries and redistribute them at random to the class. Tell them that they have found this diary entry from a celebrity and that they are going to read it. When students have read the entries, they mingle together and tell each other about what their celebrity said. Remind the students to refer to page 40 of the book if necessary, as they will have to practise their reported speech too.

Homework
Workbook p.34 Ex.1–3
Key p.104

Are you going out with Rob at the moment? pages 68–69

Warm-up

- Write *texting* and *calling* on the board and ask the class what you are referring to. Elicit that you are referring to mobile phones.
- In pairs, students think of the advantages and disadvantages of texting over calling. Allow them about two or three minutes to think of ideas.
- When they are ready, put their ideas on the board. What is the general opinion of the class?

8

- Draw students' attention to the photos and ask them who they can see. Elicit that Emily and Lisa are in the garden. Ask them if they can guess what they might be talking about and elicit that they could be talking about Rob.
- Play the recording. Students listen and read the dialogue.

Transcript 🔘 2.16

See Student's Book page 68.

LEARN IT! USE IT! TRANSLATE IT! Remind the students of these expressions in the dialogue. Check understanding by asking them to give you the equivalent expressions in their language.

9 Comprehension check

- Students read the text again and answer the questions. They check their answers in pairs. Check answers as a class.
- Ask the students to think of a few adjectives to describe Lisa and elicit any suggestions. Explain any new vocabulary. For example, *mean, sneaky, sly, nasty, dishonest* etc.

KEY
1 Maybe she is still interested in him.
2 No. She's trying to read.
3 Perhaps she wants to get away from Lisa.
4 Rob texts her.
5 She replies to Rob's message and then deletes it.
6 No, she doesn't.

Grammar Guide • Questions revision • different tenses

- Ask students what auxiliary verbs are and elicit that they are verbs to help the main verbs in different tenses. Ask them when we use them most often and elicit that they are always used in questions and interrogatives. Elicit that the three auxiliary verbs are *be, do* and *have*.
- Refer students to the list of tenses and ask them to identify the auxiliary that is being used in each one. Point out that *will* is not an auxiliary verb, but that it is a modal verb we use with the future.
- Make sure students understand the structure of the questions in each tense.

10 Check!

- Students make questions to match the answers. Remind them to look at the tense of the answers carefully before they form their questions.

- They check answers in pairs. Check answers as a class.

KEY
2 Have you seen Robin this morning?
3 What did you do last night?
4 What were you doing when Jan phoned?
5 What are you doing at the moment?
6 What are you going to do next year?
7 Do you like Chinese food?
8 What will you do when you leave school?

11 What's your secret?

- Remind students about diaries. Ask them whether they would let anybody else read their diary if they had one. Get some feedback from the class.
- Read the instructions with the students and make sure they understand that they should write each question in a different tense. Encourage them to be creative, but try to make sure they don't get too personal with their questions. Point out that, if they like, they can pretend to be somebody else as they answer the questions.
- Monitor, helping out as necessary. Make sure students are forming their sentences correctly and that they are answered in the appropriate tense.
- Get some feedback from a few pairs.

Extension

Individual writing: If only I could ask…

Tell students to think of a famous person that they really admire. It could be a sportsperson, a film star or a musician. Explain that their celebrity has agreed to answer anything they like. Ask students to make six questions using the different tenses in exercise 11.

Monitor the students as they work and make sure they are forming the questions and using the tenses correctly.

Get some feedback by asking a couple of students to read out one or two of their questions. Which questions were the most interesting?

---

12 Texting

- Ask the class if they use complete words when they send texts in their own language. Get some feedback and encourage them to think of any reasons for writing a shorter version of words.
- Explain that, in English, it is very common among young people to abbreviate their text messages. It is done by using numbers, symbols or shortened forms to represent commonly used words.
- Refer them to the images of texts and point out the questions on the left and the answers on the right. In pairs, they match them together by trying to guess what the words and symbols might mean.
- Refer them to the glossary at the bottom of the page to help them if necessary. Check answers as a class.
- Emphasise that these abbreviations are acceptable in texts to friends and people we know well. It is not acceptable to use them in other contexts such as in schoolwork, exams, formal letters or formal emails.
- Students work in pairs and 'send' each other text messages, using small pieces of paper to simulate messages going to and fro.

1 c 2 a 3 d 4 e 5 b

Extensions

Pair work: He texted to say that…

Students work in pairs. Ask them to choose two characters from the photo story. Refer them to page 4 of the book to refresh their memories if necessary.

Each student should take on the role of one of the characters. They should then take turns to text each other about something that they are planning to do, e.g. go out, do something over the weekend, etc. Encourage them to exchange about three texts each and to use the language for texting.

When they have finished, choose a pair or two to read out their text message exchange for the rest of the class.

Whole class: general knowledge quiz

Students work in pairs. Assign each pair a general category, e.g. geography, celebrity, sports etc. Ask students to make three general knowledge questions related to their category. Each of their questions should be in a different tense. Monitor, helping out with ideas and vocabulary as necessary.

When each pair is ready, explain that they are going to have a quiz on their general knowledge. Each pair works as a team and they should get some paper ready. One pair begins by asking their questions, then the next pair takes over with their lot of questions and so on until each pair has finished. Meanwhile, the other students in the class have to listen carefully to the questions and write down the answer if they know it. They are allowed to confer with their partners, but remind them to do it as quietly as possible so nobody else hears their answers.

When the quiz has finished, each pair swaps their answer sheets. Go through the correct answers and find out which pair is the brightest in the class.

Homework

Workbook p.35 Ex.4&6 & p.37 Ex.11
Key pp.104–105

I'm used to competitions   page 70

13

- Draw students' attention to the photo and ask them who they see. Elicit that Steve and Sophie are in the photo. Ask them how they look and elicit that they are dressed formally.

- Refer students to the sentences and allow them time to read them. Play the recording. Students decide if they are true or false. They check answers in pairs.

- Play the recording a second time to check answers as a class.

Transcript 2.17

Steve Hi, I'm Steve Chang.

Sophie Hello, Steve. I'm Sophie MacDonald – you've probably heard of me.

Steve Yes, my friend Amar mentioned you.

Sophie Amar… Amar… Oh, him! Yes, I remember speaking to him once. Nice guy! He's got no chance of winning the competition, though.

Steve Oh… Don't you think so?

Sophie No, I don't. In fact, I'm pretty sure I've got it sewn up, actually.

Steve How can you be so sure?

Sophie Well, I'm used to competitions, and I'm used to winning them, too.

Steve Really!

Sophie Yes, I started when I was about eight years old. I used to enter writing competitions when I was still at primary school…

Steve Did you use to win them?

Sophie Yes, I did. Of course.

Steve Amazing! And are you used to annoying the other competitors?

Sophie Er… No, I'm not. What do you mean?

Steve I mean that I've never met anyone as arrogant as you in my life.

Sophie Oh… Listen! I'm not used to people talking to me like that!

Steve Well, too bad! You'll have to get used to it if you don't change your attitude. Oh, and good luck with the competition. You'll need it!

Sophie Huh… what a strange guy!

1 F: He hasn't met her before.
2 F: She thinks he doesn't have a chance of winning.
3 T.
4 T.
5 F: He is quite rude to her.
6 F: He doesn't want her to win at all.

LEARN IT! USE IT! TRANSLATE IT! Remind the students of these expressions in the dialogue. Check understanding by asking them to give you the equivalent expressions in their language.

Grammar Guide • *be used to*

- Write the following sentence on the board: *I'm used to competitions*. Ask the students who says it in the dialogue, Steve or Sophie. Elicit that Sophie says it. Ask them what she means and elicit that she has done many competitions before so she knows how they work and she knows how to approach them. They are not unusual for her so she is used to them.

- Point out the structure of *be used to* and make sure students understand the different forms in the affirmative, negative and interrogative.

- Now write the following sentence on the board: *I used to enter competitions when I was still at primary school*. Ask the students who says this and elicit that it is Sophie. Ask them what she means and elicit that she entered competitions regularly when she was a child. Emphasise that in this case, *used to* is the past tense that we use to talk about past habits (see Student's Book page 7).

- Make sure students understand the difference in meaning and the different structures between *used to do* and *be used to doing*.

LOOK OUT! When we are accustomed to doing something we *are used to* it. However, in many cases it takes some time to become accustomed to something. For example: *John was used to driving on the right hand side of the road in the USA. When he came to the UK, he spent two weeks getting used to driving on the other side of the road. Now, he is used to it.*

Point out that, in general, we use *be used to* when the process of *getting used to* is complete.

14 Check!

- Draw students' attention to the incomplete sentences and ask them to complete them with either *used to* (past habits) or *be used to* (familiar with something).
- They check answers in pairs. Check answers as a class.

KEY
1 We're used to getting
2 I didn't use to walk
3 I'm used to studying
4 Did you use to go
5 Are they used to speaking
6 You're used to playing

15 The summer's different!

- Ask the students to think of their two favourite things about the summer holidays. Allow them to discuss in pairs for a minute or two. Get some feedback from the class.
- Read the instructions with the class and explain that each of their sentences should contain *be used to*. They write their sentences. Monitor, checking that they are forming their sentences correctly.
- When they are ready, they swap their sentences and identify which of their partner's are false. Get some feedback from the class.

ALREADY FINISHED? Read the instructions for the writing activity with the students. Point out that they should try to use a variety of tenses, but that they should be careful that they flow together naturally. The activity can be set for homework.

Homework
Workbook p.36 Ex.8–10
Key p.104

Grammar Check page 71

Phrasal verbs

1
Type 1: adverb…object
Type 2: preposition…pronoun
Type 3: object
Type 4: verb…preposition

2
1 away 2 away 3 with 4 off 5 up 6 forward to

Verb tense revision

3
1 Present simple 2 Present continuous 3 Past simple
4 Present perfect 5 Past continuous 6 will
7 be going to 8 Past perfect

4
1 will be 2 was just coming in 3 spend
4 were driving 5 'm going to 6 'm listening

5
1 Have you ever been to England?
2 Do you like studying English?
3 Are you reading any English books at the moment?
4 Did you get good marks last year in English?
5 Are you going (to go) to an English-speaking country this summer?
6 Do you think English will be the world's most common language in 50 years' time?

be used to/get used to/used to

6
1 used to 2 get used to 3 be used to

7
1 I'm used to going to school on foot.
2 When I was ten, I used to go swimming every Saturday, but I don't go now.
3 I'm not used to eating sushi.
4 Are you used to spending Christmas at home?
5 She didn't use to go abroad on holiday when she was younger.
6 Did you use to live in London before you moved?

Homework
Workbook p.35 Ex.5 & p.36 Ex.7 & p.37 Revision
Key pp.104–105

Skills and culture pages 72–73

Warm-up

- Ask the students to imagine what their life would be like if they didn't have their mobile phones. In pairs, they think of three reasons why they would miss them.
- Get some feedback from the class. Is there anybody who wouldn't miss them?

1 Speaking

- Draw students' attention to the pictures of the different devices on the right hand side of the page. They match them with the words in the box.
- In pairs, students check their answers. They rank the items from the most useful to the least useful. Encourage them to discuss each item as they rank it.
- When they are ready, they join other pairs in the class and compare their top three most useful devices. Encourage them to explain their reasons for choosing these devices. Monitor, helping out with vocabulary or ideas as necessary.
- Get feedback from the class by getting them to agree on the top three most useful devices.

1 calculator   **2** TV   **3** digital camera   **4** DVD player
5 Sat Nav   **6** mobile   **7** laptop   **8** modem   **9** MP3
player   **10** games console

2 Reading

- Refer students to the text and ask them to skim-read it to find out whether Steve is in favour of or against technology. Remind them to focus on understanding the main idea.

- After about two minutes, stop the students and elicit that Steve is neither for nor against technology. He discusses both sides of the argument, but he does not choose one.

3

- Ask the students what technological devices Steve discusses in his article and elicit that he talks about mobiles and the Internet.

- Draw their attention to the structure of the text. Point out that there are six paragraphs. The first one is an introduction and the last one is the conclusion. The four paragraphs in between are discussing mobile phones and the Internet. Elicit that each device has two paragraphs each, and that one of these paragraphs discusses the disadvantages while the other discusses the advantages.

- Point out that, in general, it is useful to identify how texts are structured as it makes it easier to locate relevant information.

- Refer students to the chart and ask them to complete it with information from the text for each column. They check answers in pairs. Check answers as a class.

mobile phones: for
can call dad to pick up when no buses
can save lives when accident
mobile phones: against
often intrusive (loud use in public)
possible health problems from electromagnetic waves
make spelling and grammar worse
make people antisocial
the Internet: for
can work from home
keeping in touch with people made easy
easy to get answers and information
the Internet: against
children having problems concentrating at school
less time spent reading books
too much information that can't be absorbed
physical problems from sitting, staring and typing too much

4

- Remind students that building their vocabulary is always important and that it is an ongoing process. They should always be adding to their existing knowledge and they should take advantage of reading texts to do so.

- Explain the task. Students work individually and identify six new words, including a phrasal verb. They then try to work out their meanings from their context.

- When they are ready they work in pairs. They compare their lists and help each other by deciding if they agree or

disagree with their partner's definitions. Refer them to a dictionary to check their answers.

Students' own answers.

5 Listening

- Ask for a show of hands from the class to see how many people regularly play computer games. Get feedback from any students who raise their hands. Ask what kind of games they play and how often they play them.

- Explain that they are going to listen to a conversation about computer games. Play the recording. Students answer the question.

- Remind students about the chart they completed in exercise 3. Ask them to draw a similar chart for computer games with a *for* and an *against* column.

- Play the recording a second time. Students make notes on the advantages and disadvantages of computer games according to the speakers. They check their notes in pairs.

- If you feel it is necessary, play the recording a third time for students to check their notes and add anything they didn't hear before. Check answers as a class.

Transcript 🔊 2.18

Daisy Oh, Cory! You're playing computer games again!
Cory Hang on a minute, I've nearly finished this level. There! So what's the problem?
Daisy Well, you spend hours playing them.
Cory So? I find it helps me relax when I've finished doing my homework.
Daisy The trouble is, you're used to playing them every evening, and you've got important exams this June – you must be playing computer games instead of studying.
Cory That's not true! I always wait until I've finished all my homework. Anyway, there are lots of good reasons for playing.
Daisy Like what?
Cory It improves your reflexes for one thing. I used to be much slower. When I learn to drive next year, I'll be able to react faster in an emergency.
Daisy Well, I suppose that's something. But that's the only good thing.
Cory No – if you play strategy games, you develop the ability to solve problems, consider arguments and make decisions, too.
Daisy Mmm… But don't you think it would be more interesting to go out with your friends?
Cory I go out with my friends a lot. Sometimes I just want to be on my own – and it's cheaper to stay at home playing than going out.
Daisy That's not really true! Those games cost a fortune!
Cory Yes, you're right there – but they're really exciting!
Daisy Yes, exciting and violent, too. I mean, some of them have been banned, they're so violent.
Cory Not the ones I play.
Daisy It must be bad for your eyes, though, staring at that screen for hours.
Cory Well, that is true – I think you have to be careful not to play for too long or you can get a headache. But you're the one who's got glasses, not me. Maybe you spend too much time reading!
Daisy Ha ha! Very funny!

Cory Anyway – do you want to have a go? I've got a second controller here.

Daisy Go on then. Let's see if it's as amazing as you say…

KEY

Cory changes Daisy's mind more.
Students' own answers.

6 Speaking

- Divide students into groups of four and explain that each person should choose a different device from exercise 1. Individually, they make a similar chart to the ones from exercise 3 and 5 in which they make notes in favour of and against their chosen device. Remind them that their notes should not necessarily be full sentences and that they will just be using them to help them remember their ideas.

- Monitor as the students formulate their ideas, helping out where necessary.

- When they are ready, they tell the rest of the group about their device explaining why they are in favour of it. Encourage the other students to make their own notes as they listen and to then argue against the student who was speaking.

- Monitor, making sure that students are not only participating, but allowing each other time to speak and make their opinions clear.

- When the activity is finished, students have a vote on who made the most convincing speech.

> **STUDY STRATEGY** 'For and against' essays are very common and are often used in English exams. It is not only important to have a clear opinion on the topic, but you must also be able to discuss the other point of view too, using examples to support each side.
> Once you have a clear list of ideas to use, it is very useful to make a rough plan of what you want to say and to follow the standard structure for writing this type of essay. Plans make sure that you stay focused on the topic and that you don't forget to include a good idea you might have thought of.
> Read through the steps with the class and make sure they understand the logic behind the steps.

7 Writing

- Tell students to choose one of the devices from exercise 1. If they like, they can choose the same device they chose in exercise 6.

- Read through the instructions with the class and read the Study Strategy with them. Draw their attention to the four points that they should include in their essay.

- Allow them some time to brainstorm ideas and to organise them into a rough plan. Remind them that it is important to leave themselves some time to check their writing for any grammar or spelling mistakes they may have made.

- The activity may be set for homework.

Extension
Language plus p.98

Exam plus 7

Listening • Multiple-choice page 74

Warm-up

- Students work in pairs. Ask them to imagine that they are starting university for the first time and will be living away from home. They think of three things they are looking forward to and three things that they are nervous about.

- After about three minutes, stop the students. Get feedback from each pair and put their ideas on the board.

1

- Read the instructions with the class and make sure they understand the task. Explain that they will hear the recording twice. During the first listening, they should answer the question in exercise 1. They should also familiarise themselves with the recording and identify the relevant sections in which they can find their answers.

- Draw students' attention to questions 1–6 in exercise 2 and allow them time to read the questions and options carefully. As always, they should identify key words to help them focus on the recording.

- Play the recording. Remind students to think about the questions in exercise 2 as they listen. Students answer the question in exercise 1 and check their answers in pairs. Check answers as a class.

Transcript 🔊 2.19

Reporter Hello. Can I ask you a few questions for our magazine? We'd like to find out about student life in Bristol.
Sally OK, why not?
Reporter What's your name and where are you from?
Sally My name's Sally, Sally Thompson, and I moved here from Kilburn in London.
Reporter What are you studying?
Sally I'm studying English at Bristol University.
Reporter Where do you live? Do you live in halls of residence?
Sally No, I don't. I live in a shared flat on Gloucester Road. At first, I found it difficult to get used to sharing a flat with other students because I was used to having my family around, but I think it's OK now.
Reporter Is there anything you don't like about it?
Sally I'm not used to cooking my own meals. My mum used to do all the cooking for me when I was at home.
Reporter And what do you like about sharing a flat?
Sally There are five of us, so it's easier to do the housework. We can always help each other.
Reporter How do you get to university?
Sally Now that's something that was unusual for me, coming from London. I'm not really used to walking to lectures from home. You can't do that in London because the city is so big, you have to take the Tube if you want to go anywhere.
Reporter And how's it going at college?

Sally Great. The lecturers are really nice, and my subject is quite interesting. Most of my lectures are in the afternoon, so I can often sleep until late, which is a good thing because I had to get used to studying late in the library. When I was at home, my evenings were free, but here I've got too much on for that.
Reporter And what about your social life?
Sally Well, I've never been a party girl, and I'm not used to going clubbing on Saturdays, which most of the other students do almost every week here. I still prefer going out for a nice meal, or staying in to watch a film on video or something.
Reporter But all in all, are you enjoying student life in Bristol?
Sally Yes, I am. I think it's great.
Reporter Thanks for talking to us, Sally.

KEY
c

2

- Remind students that they should listen more carefully to the recording and focus on the relevant sections where they will find their answers.

- Point out that they will often hear synonyms instead of the words that are in the questions.

- To help prepare students for the task, you may like to ask them to read the questions and options carefully, then elicit a few different ways the statements in the options could be phrased. Being able to paraphrase (and to recognise in paraphrased variants) the same information is the key to how listening comprehension tasks work in exams.

- Play the recording a second time. Students check their answers in pairs. Check answers as a class. If you feel the students would benefit from it, play the recording a third time as you check their answers so they understand why the options are correct.

Transcript 🔊 2.19
See exercise 1 above.

KEY
1 c **2** b **3** a **4** a **5** b **6** c

> **EXAM TIP** Students should maximise their time before a listening to read the different questions and options, identifying key words and thinking about what they might hear. During the first listening, they should familiarise themselves as much as they can with the text, so that as they listen the second time, they have a good idea of what they should focus on for the answers.

Use of English • Key word transformation page 74

3

- Write the following two sentences on the board: *When I was a child, I used to go to the beach every summer.* and *I went to the beach every summer during my childhood.* Ask the class to look at the two sentences and ask them what the difference in meaning is. Elicit that there is no difference in meaning and that the sentences are simply structured in a different way.

- Point out that in this task, the students have to be able to say the same thing in a different way. Read the instructions with the class and make sure they understand the task.
- Do the first one together with the class. Read the first sentence and check that students understand that James is familiar with driving on the right hand side of the road as he has always done so. Draw their attention to the incomplete sentence and to the keyword. Point out that they must use the key word without changing it.
- Ask the class if they can use *used* in any way to mean that you are familiar with something and elicit that we can use the structure *be used to*. Focus their attention on the gap and elicit that we need to insert *is used to driving* in order to complete it correctly.
- Students complete the rest of the task and check their answers in pairs. Check answers as a class.

KEY

1 is used to driving
2 studies hard, she will
3 will be announced
4 I would have watched
5 was so difficult
6 when/after she had finished
7 that she was going
8 used to go

EXAM TIP Students need to compare the first sentence with the incomplete second sentence carefully to identify exactly what kind of structure they will need to complete it. Point out that the meaning must be the same: if they complete the sentence with correct grammar but with a different meaning, they will not get the marks.

Further exam practice
Workbook pp.42–43

Exam plus 8

Objectives
To practise exams related to the material covered in Unit 8
Reading: Sentence completion
Writing: Article
Speaking: Guided conversation

Reading • Sentence completion page 75

Warm-up
- Students work in pairs. Ask them to think about ways they can spend their money while benefiting other people at the same time. Allow them a few minutes to compare ideas.
- When they are ready, get feedback from the class. Put their ideas on the board for everyone to see.

1
- Read the instructions with the students. Ask them to skim-read the article to find out what the purpose of *The Big Issue* is. Elicit that it is a magazine that is sold by people who are homeless and that all of the profits are for their benefit.
- Draw students' attention to the incomplete sentences at the bottom of the page. Explain that in this task, they must use one word to complete each sentence. They need to read each sentence carefully and compare it with the original text so that they can identify what word they need to complete it.
- Point out that they should first identify what kind of word (noun, verb, adjective etc.) they need.
- Do the first one with the class as an example. Read the first statement and then ask the students to underline the part of the text that contains the same information. Elicit that it is the first sentence of the text. Ask the class what kind of word they need for the first statement and elicit that they need a noun, probably related to time. Ask them if there is any reference to time in the first sentence of the text and elicit that the word *weekly* refers to time. Explain that this is an adverb, while the students need a noun. Elicit that *week* is the correct answer.
- Students complete the rest of the statements by themselves. They check answers in pairs. Check answers as a class.

KEY
1 week   2 stars   3 businessman   4 homeless
5 prove   6 copy   7 successful

EXAM TIP Point out the importance of comparing the statements with the text carefully. This will allow the students to identify which piece of information is missing and then help them to decide on the missing word.

Writing • Article page 75

2
- Read the instructions with the students carefully and draw their attention to the information that they are asked to include.

- Allow them some time to think of what they are going to write about. If you like, divide them into pairs and encourage them to swap ideas about popular events. Remind students that they should always do a quick brainstorm to get their ideas together before they begin to write. They should then plan their articles.
- Students write their articles. Point out that they should leave enough time at the end of the activity to go back and check their work for mistakes in spelling and grammar that they may have made.

> **EXAM TIP** Point out the different sections to an article and remind students to plan their articles before they begin to write them. Refer them to page 73 to see how an article can be planned and then developed.

Speaking • Guided conversation page 75

3

- Read the task with the students and go through the questions with them.
- Point out that they should try to develop their answers as much as possible. It is important for them to support their answers as it gives them a chance to show the examiner what they can do. Remind them that it is not important if they don't really mean what they say – the purpose of the speaking exam is to assess speaking, not opinion.
- Allow students a little time to think about the questions and what they are going to say. Encourage them to make notes to help them, but make sure they don't try to write full sentences.
- Divide students into pairs. They do the task. Monitor them as they speak. Keep interruptions to a minimum: if students are speaking don't try to correct any mistakes at this stage. If students are struggling, help out with ideas or vocabulary as necessary.
- When students have finished, choose a few stronger students to perform the task for the rest of the class.

> **EXAM TIP** Emphasise the importance of developing answers as much as possible. Giving examples and speculating are good ways to keep the students speaking if they are not sure what to say. They are being examined on their ability to speak and not on what they actually say.

Further exam practice
Workbook pp.42–43

Topic and vocabulary

Life choices

Regrets

Shopping

Consumerist society

Grammar

Third conditional

Conditionals revision

wish + Past perfect

Functions

Imagining a different past

Talking about regrets

Skills and culture/pronunciation

Speaking: talking about experiences and opinions, speculating about the future

Reading: predicting content, general comprehension, matching definitions

Listening: multiple-choice statements

Writing: finishing a story

Pronunciation: *c* + vowel

Estimated time: 7–8 hours

If I'd known, I'd have called pages 76–77

Warm-up

- Write the word *regret* on the board and ask the class what it means. Elicit that a regret is something that we did in the past that we feel sorry about and that we would like to change if we had the opportunity to do so. Point out that it is also a verb.

- Ask the class to think of one regret each and to then compare it with their partner. Get feedback by asking a few students to describe their partner's regret.

1

- Refer the class to the photos at the top of the page. Allow them a little while to look at the people and what they're doing. Ask them how they think Amar looks and elicit that he looks hopeful and nervous. Ask them where they think the people are and elicit that they are probably at the final ceremony of the IYJC.

- Ask them what they think is happening to Rob and Emily and elicit that they seem to be arguing. Ask them how Lisa looks and elicit that she looks like she regrets something.

- Students read and listen to the conversation.

Transcript 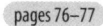 2.20

See Student's Book page 76.

LEARN IT! USE IT! TRANSLATE IT! Ask the students to find the expressions in the text. Check understanding by asking them to give you the equivalent expressions in their language.

2 Comprehension check

- Students read the text again and answer the questions. Check answers as a class.

- Ask the class what they think Lisa should do to make things better for Rob and Emily and accept any suggestions the students make.

KEY

1 No, he isn't happy to see her.
2 She thought he'd decided not to come.
3 He shows her the text he thought Emily had sent.
4 Yes, he does.
5 She thinks Amar will win it.
6 He thinks Sophie MacDonald will win.

Extension

Group work: Who is going to win?

Divide students into groups. Explain that they are about to find out who is going to win the IYJC.

In their groups, students discuss each of the candidates and decide who they think is going to win. Encourage them to listen to each other's suggestions and reasons before they agree on a final winner. Monitor, helping out as necessary.

Get feedback from each group, putting their suggestions on the board before moving on to the next exercise.

3 Listening

- Play the recording. Students listen to the announcement and identify the winner. Check the answer as a class.

- In pairs, students briefly discuss whether they agree with the result. If they disagree, encourage them to explain their opinion. Get feedback from a few pairs.

Transcript 2.21

Mr Martins And the winner of this year's International Young Journalist Competition is… Amar Prabhu! Come up here, Amar.

Jackie Well done, Amar.

Steve Yeah, congratulations!

Amar Oh, thanks, everyone. I just can't believe it!

Rebecca Go on, Amar. Get up there.

KEY

Amar Prabhu is the winner of the IYJC.

Grammar Guide • Third conditional

- Draw students' attention to the conversation in exercise 1 again and refer them to Rob's statement *If Steve hadn't invited me, I wouldn't have come.*

- Ask the students if Rob came to the ceremony and elicit that he did. Ask them why he came and elicit that Steve invited him. Write these two sentences on the board: *Steve invited Rob. He came to the ceremony.*

- As a class, compare these two sentences with Rob's statement in the text. Explain that Rob is talking about what would have been different if something else had happened. He is talking about an imaginary past which cannot be changed. This is the Third conditional.
- Go through the forms of the structure and make sure the class understand them. Ask them to look through the conversation and to underline any more Third conditional forms that they can find.

4 Check!

- Students complete the sentences with the subject and correct form of the verbs. Remind them to think carefully about which part of the sentence they are completing so that they use the correct structures.
- They check answers in pairs. Check answers as a class.

KEY

1 I'd remembered   2 I'd stayed   3 I'd saved
4 would you have done   5 I wouldn't have rented
6 she had spent   7 would they have done
8 he wouldn't have had

Extension

Pair work: Why did it happen?

Refer students to the cartoon at the bottom of the page and elicit that it is a picture of a car accident.

In their pairs, they think of five possible reasons for the crash. For example, *He wasn't driving carefully; He didn't see the sign; The girl was talking to him; They were having an argument; He hadn't checked the car.* Monitor, helping out with ideas or vocabulary as necessary.

When the students are ready, they make conditional sentences using their reasons. For example, *If he had been driving carefully, he wouldn't have crashed the car.* Monitor, checking that they are forming their sentences correctly.

When students have finished, ask each pair to read out one of their sentences for the rest of the class.

---

5 If it hadn't happened…

- Draw students' attention to the photo of Bill Gates and elicit who he is. Allow the students one or two minutes to tell you what they know about him. Would any of them like to be him?
- Explain the task to the class. Point out the three lists of information and explain that they can be matched together to make conditional sentences. Draw their attention to the example sentence.
- In pairs, ask the students to work in pairs to match the information together before they make their conditional sentences. Monitor to check that they have the correct combinations before they start to change the verbs.
- Individually, students write the sentences using the correct forms. Monitor, helping out as necessary. They check their answers in pairs. Check answers as a class.
- In pairs, students discuss whether or not they agree with the sentences. Get feedback from the class.

KEY

2 If Bill Gates hadn't started Microsoft, he wouldn't have become the richest man in the world.

---

3 If Germany hadn't invaded Poland, the Second World War wouldn't have started.
4 If photographers hadn't followed Princess Diana, she wouldn't have died in a car crash.
5 If the Pope had given Henry VIII a divorce, England wouldn't have become Protestant.
6 If there hadn't been famine in Ethiopia, Bob Geldof wouldn't have organised Live Aid.

> **CULTURE NOTE** **Bill Gates** is a famous American businessman who started the software company Microsoft. He is one of the richest men in the world, even though he didn't finish his university degree. He started Microsoft in 1975, at the age of twenty. He has donated a considerable part of his wealth to various charities.

6 What would you have done?

- Remind students that the Third conditional is used to describe an imaginary past and to talk about what would have been different so we often use it to talk about regrets. Remind them of the regrets they thought about at the beginning of the unit.
- Students write six Third conditional sentences about their own life. Point out that they can include the two regrets they thought about at the start of the unit. Monitor, helping out with ideas and vocabulary as necessary and checking that they are forming their sentences correctly.
- When they have finished, they work in pairs. Taking turns, they should read the first half of their sentences so that their partner can continue by guessing what would have happened. Monitor, listening out for correct use of the Third conditional.
- At the end of the activity, get some feedback from a few pairs.

Extension

Pair work: Let's save the world

Have a brainstorming session with the class by asking them to think of various world problems. These can be related to the environment or to political situations.

When you have their ideas on the board, ask them to think of reasons why these problems might have happened. They should make Third conditional sentences to describe each situation. For example, *If people hadn't used so much fossil fuel, the ice at the North Pole wouldn't have melted so much.*

Get some feedback from each pair. Do the rest of the class agree with their suggestions?

Homework
Workbook p.38 Ex.2–4
Key p.105

If I were you, I'd forget about it

pages 78–79

Warm-up

- Students work in pairs. Ask them to briefly discuss what their main ambition in life is.

- Get some feedback from the class and put any new vocabulary on the board for everyone to see.

7

- Draw students' attention to the photos and ask them to tell you what they think Rob and Emily are talking about. Elicit any acceptable responses.
- Play the recording. Students listen and read the dialogue.

Transcript 🔘 2.22

See Student's Book page 78.

LEARN IT! USE IT! TRANSLATE IT! Remind the students of these expressions in the dialogue. Check understanding by asking them to give you the equivalent expressions in their language.

8 Comprehension check

- Students read the text again and decide if the statements are true or false. They check their answers in pairs. Check answers as a class.
- Ask the students to look at Lorenzo and Sophie in the photo. Ask: *How do you think they are feeling? Who are they looking at?* (Lorenzo's looking at Emily. Sophie's looking at Amar.)

KEY
1 T.
2 T.
3 F: He thought she wasn't a very good friend to Emily.
4 T.
5 F: He thinks he wasn't exciting enough.
6 F: She's completely over Lorenzo.

Grammar Guide • Conditionals revision

- Ask the class what a conditional sentence is and elicit that it is a sentence that has two clauses. One clause (the *if* clause) makes a condition, while the other clause says the result of that condition.
- Ask the class how many types of conditionals they have seen and elicit that they have seen three. Refer them to the dialogues in exercise 7 and ask them to identify one of each type. Check answers as a class.
- Go through the different structures for each type of conditional and make sure they can see the differences between each one.
- Check that they understand the differences in their uses. The First conditional is used to talk about possible situations in the present and in the future. The Second conditional is used to talk about unlikely situations in the present and in the future. It is also used to talk about imaginary situations in the present. The Third conditional is used to talk about imaginary situations in the past.

9 Check!

- Students match the sentence halves together to form correct sentences. When they have finished, ask them to identify what kind of conditional each sentence is.
- They check answers in pairs. Check answers as a class.

KEY
1 f (First)   2 h (Third)   3 d (Second)   4 a (Third)
5 c (Second)   6 b (First)   7 e (Third)   8 g (Third)

10 Vocabulary • life choices

- Refer students to the diagram and explain that it is a mind map. Allow them time to copy it into their exercise books.
- Ask them what they think a mind map is and elicit that it is a useful method of recording vocabulary. The main topic is in the centre of the diagram and the subtopics are connected to it.
- Explain that they have to organise the vocabulary into the appropriate categories. They do the task and check their answers in pairs. Check the answers as a class.
- Encourage them to think of some more life choices to add to each category. Put their suggestions on the board.

KEY
Family life: get engaged, have a baby, stay single, get married, leave home, settle down
Study: have a gap year, apply for university, go to university, study abroad, get a degree
Work: have an interview, apply for a job, be unemployed, start a company, get a job
Accommodation: rent a house/flat, share a house/flat, live at home, buy a house/flat

---

Extension

Pair work: collocations

Refer students to the list of life choices in exercise 10. Point out that most of the phrases contain a verb and a noun/adjective. Explain that these verbs should not be mixed up and that they are known as collocations (they naturally occur together).

Students have two minutes to study the list. Explain that they should try to memorise as many of the phrases as possible. Ask them to close their books.

They work in pairs. Say a noun or adjective to the class, e.g. *degree*. In their pairs, students write down *get a degree*. Continue the activity by saying another nine nouns or adjectives form the list (some of them will match with more than one verb). When you have finished, ask students to check their answers in the book. How many pairs got all of the collocations correct?

---

11 If everything goes well…

- Read the task with the students and make sure they understand what they have to do. Point out that they should look carefully at the beginning of the sentence so that they know which conditional they have to use in order to complete it correctly.
- Working individually, students complete the sentences. Monitor the activity to make sure they are using the vocabulary effectively and that they are forming the conditional sentences correctly.
- When they have finished, they compare their sentences in pairs. Get some feedback from a few pairs.

KEY
Students' own answers.

Homework
Workbook p.38 Ex.1 & p.39–40 Ex.5–8
Key pp.105–106

I wish I hadn't done it! page 80

12

- Draw students' attention to the photo and ask them who they see. Elicit that Steve, Jackie, Amar and Rebecca are talking to Lisa. Ask them how Lisa looks and elicit vocabulary such as *regretful, miserable, sad*, etc.
- Refer students to the questions and allow them time to read them. Play the recording. Students answer the questions and check their answers in pairs.
- Play the recording a second time to check answers as a class.

Transcript 🔊 2.23

Steve You shouldn't have messed around with Emily's messages, Lisa. It was really out of order.

Lisa I know, don't tell me! I'm so sorry. I can't believe how awful I was. I wish I hadn't done it.

Steve I think you ought to apologise to Emily and Rob.

Lisa Yes, I will, don't worry. I wish I hadn't been so stupid. I don't know what I was thinking. I was just jealous and upset, but that's no excuse.

Amar Well, I suppose we all make mistakes.

Steve At least Rob and Emily are back together again – no thanks to you.

Lisa I should never have come to the UK. I wish I'd stayed at home and tried to sort things out with Andy.

Rebecca Don't say that, Lisa. We've really enjoyed meeting you.

Lisa Oh, thanks, Rebecca. I've had a really good time here with you all, too. I'm really sorry for what I did.

Jackie Well, all's well that ends well. And that goes for the competition too – well done, Amar!

Steve Yes, congratulations, Amar! You showed Sophie MacDonald! You're the best!

Amar Thanks, everyone! But I wouldn't have managed it without your support and friendship. Now then, let's go and celebrate. How about going for a curry?

Steve Excellent! Let's go! Come on, Lisa – come with us.

KEY

1 Yes, she is.
2 He wants her to apologise to Emily and Rob.
3 She says she should have tried to sort things out with Andy.
4 No, she isn't.
5 He thanks them for their support and friendship.
6 They're going to go for a curry.

LEARN IT! USE IT! TRANSLATE IT! Remind the students of these expressions in the dialogue. Check understanding by asking them to give you the equivalent expressions in their language.

Grammar Guide • *wish* + Past perfect

- Remind students about *wish* + Past simple (see Student's Book page 29). Ask them what it is used for and elicit that we use *wish* + Past simple to describe what we would like to be different about the present, e.g. *I wish it wasn't raining today.*
- Draw their attention to the title of the lesson, *I wish I hadn't done it*, and ask them who says this. Elicit that Lisa says this. Explain that she is talking about the past. In a similar way to the Third conditional, we use *wish* + Past perfect to

describe how we would like the past to be different. We cannot change it, so we are expressing our regret about a situation.

- Go through the different structures with the class and make sure they understand them.

13 Check!

- Draw students' attention to the situations and allow them time to read through them. Point out that in each one, the person wishes they had done something differently.
- Students rewrite the sentences using *wish* + Past perfect. Point out that the meaning will be the same. They check answers in pairs. Check answers as a class.

KEY

1 Mike wishes he hadn't had a tattoo done.
2 I wish I hadn't stayed out very late last night.
3 We wish it hadn't rained all the time.
4 He wishes he hadn't left home late and missed the plane.
5 I wish I hadn't been late for class.
6 She wishes she hadn't left home last year.

Extension

Pair work: I wish it had been different…

Tell students to think about their lives as students and ask them to imagine five things in the past that would have made the experience better or easier for them. Encourage them to use *wish* + Past perfect to describe their ideas. For example, *I wish exams had never been invented.*

Monitor the students as they work, helping out with vocabulary or ideas where necessary. When the students have finished, get some ideas from each pair. Which pair has the best ideas?

---

14 I wish I'd…

- Explain that the students are going to listen to six situations. They have to write down what each person wishes.
- Draw their attention to the vocabulary in the box and allow them time to look through it. Play the first situation and pause the recording. Refer students to the example.
- Play the remaining situations. Pause after each to allow students time to decide on the vocabulary they need and to make their sentences.
- Play the recording a second time to allow students time to check their answers. Check answers as a class. Ask them which situation they would hate to be in the most and get some ideas from one or two students.

Transcript 🔊 2.24

1 Oh no, they've scored. They've won.
2 Aaargh!
3 Oh no! It's gone!
4 Oh no! My car!
5 Oh no, where have I put them? Oh, I haven't got them… Oh, I can't believe it – there's no one at home!
6 **TV Presenter** So, those winning numbers are: 4, 8, 15, 16, 23 and 42! Are you the lucky winner of 4.2 million pounds?
   Woman I've won! I've won! Oh no! I can't find the ticket. Where did I put it?

2 I wish I hadn't hit my thumb.
3 I wish I hadn't missed the train.
4 I wish I hadn't driven so fast.
5 I wish I hadn't lost my keys.
6 I wish I had put the ticket somewhere safe.

ALREADY FINISHED? Students think about the *New Horizons* story and imagine what they would like to have been different. They make six sentences using *wish* + Past perfect. Encourage them to think about the competition, the characters, the relationships, etc. The activity can be set for homework.

Pronunciation • *c* + vowel

Write the letter *c* on the board. Ask the students to say the letter in English. If necessary, say it for them yourself so that they can copy you.

Explain that *c* can be pronounced in two ways, /k/ or /s/. This depends on the spelling of the word.

1 Students listen to the recording. Draw students' attention to the words. Play the recording. Students listen again and repeat. Repeat the words yourself so the students get the pronunciation properly. Ask them what the rule is.

Transcript 🔊 2.25

See Student's Book page 80.

KEY

c is pronounced /k/ when followed by the vowels *a, u* and *o*.
c is pronounced /s/ when followed by the vowels *e* and *i*.

2 Students work in pairs and look through the list of words. Encourage them to say them aloud to each other and to decide if they should pronounce the *c* as /k/ or /s/. Play the recording to check their answers. They listen and repeat.

Transcript 🔊 2.26

See Student's Book page 80.

KEY

/k/: competition, congratulations, curry, come
/s/: celebrate, receive, necessary, decide, cinema, certain

| **Homework**
| Workbook p.40–41 Ex.9–11
| Key p.106

Grammar Check (page 81)

Third conditional

1
1 Past perfect…*would have*
2 'd been…have visited
3 hadn't read…have
4 the opposite of what happened in the past

2
2 If she'd remembered to bring an umbrella, she wouldn't have got wet.
3 They would have had a better holiday if they'd gone to Spain.
4 We wouldn't have spent so much if we'd eaten pizza.

5 If I'd known about the match, I would have brought my football boots.
6 He would have won the prize if he had entered the competition.

3
Students' own answers.

Conditionals revision

4
a 1   **b** 3   **c** 2

5
Possible answers:
1 ✓
2 If you hadn't got such bad marks in the exam, we'd have given you a present.
3 If you lived in London, you would speak English very well.
4 ✓
5 If you give me £5, I'll get you a T-shirt.
6 We'll go to the seaside if the weather is better.

wish + Past perfect

6
a 2   **b** 1   **c** 1   **d** 2

7
1 I wish you hadn't eaten so much for dinner.
2 I wish my friend had invited me to her birthday party.
3 I wish I were very fit.
4 I wish I had had lunch today.
5 I wish I had learned German.
6 I wish I had had some pets when I was a child.

8
1 I wish I had gone to the dentist's.
2 I wish I hadn't gone to school by bike.
3 I wish I'd saved more money.
4 She wishes she'd stayed at school.
5 He wishes he'd had more courage.

| **Homework**
| Workbook p.41 Revision
| Key p.106

Skills and culture (pages 82–83)

Warm-up

- Write *consumerism* on the board and ask the students if they know what it means. Elicit that it refers to the way that people spend money and buy things that they want or think they want. Point out that somebody who shops is called a consumer.

- In pairs, students tell each other about the last thing they bought. Get some feedback from one or two students about their partners.

1 Speaking

- Draw students' attention to the questions and allow them some time to read through them. Check for understanding.

- They discuss the questions in their pairs. Encourage them to develop their speaking by giving reasons and examples to support their answers.
- Monitor the students as they speak, helping with vocabulary and ideas where necessary. Make a note of any errors you would like to come back to at a later time.
- Bring the activity to a close by briefly discussing each question as a class.

2 Reading

- Refer students to the title of the text. Remind them that they should use the title of any text to try to predict its content. Ask them what they think it will be about and put any ideas on the board.

3

- Ask the students what they should now do. They should be able to tell you that they have to skim-read the text for the main idea.
- Students skim-read the text and check their ideas in exercise 2.

KEY

The article talks about consumerism and raises the question of whether we actually need to buy all of the things that we do.

4

- Refer students to the questions and allow them some time to read them. Point out that they should identify key words to help them locate the relevant section of the text in which they can find their answers.
- Students answer the questions based on the text. They check their answers in pairs. Check answers as a class.

KEY

1 He says they spend their money on things that are not really necessary for survival.
2 We often buy things we don't need because advertising can influence us.
3 He says that happiness comes from what we are and how we treat other people.
4 It says that consumerism contributes to environmental problems, criminal activity and exploitation of poorer countries.
5 They say that it makes them lose their social skills and stops them from doing more constructive things.
6 We would help poorer countries when we bought things.

5

- Draw students' attention to the highlighted words and expressions in the text. At this stage they should be used to working out the meanings of words from their context in a sentence, but remind them anyway.
- Students match the words to their synonyms or definitions. They check their answers in pairs. Check answers as a class.

KEY

1 unfashionable   2 uncaring   3 majority
4 greed   5 reconsider   6 fulfilled   7 exploit
8 social skills   9 obsession   10 wages

6 Listening

- Remind the students that Amar won the IYJC and that the article they just read was considered the best by the judges. Explain that they are now going to listen to him speak at the ceremony.
- In their pairs, student think about what Amar might say in his speech. Get some ideas from each pair.
- Refer the class to the questions and their options. Allow them time to read them. Tell them that they should use them to try to predict the content of the recording.
- Play the recording. Students choose the correct options and check their answers in pairs.
- Play the recording a second time. Check answers as a class.

Transcript 🔘 2.27

Amar First of all, I'd like to thank Mr Martins, the chairman of the judges for the International Young Journalist Competition, and all the members of the panel who voted for my article. It's a great honour to have been chosen to take part in the final and an even greater honour to have won.

I believe that the competition is incredibly important for many reasons. It gives young people from around the world the chance to meet, to compare their experiences and to find out about other countries. This kind of contact makes the world a smaller and friendlier place. If people from different countries understand each other better, there's a greater chance that we'll all be able to live in harmony.

I think that was also one of the themes of my article, Think before you buy. When I came to the UK I was struck by people's materialism – the quantity of things that people possess. For a lot of people, as you know, life is very different. Although there are people in India who have just as many material possessions as people in the UK, the majority of the population there belong to the fifty per cent of the world that survives on two dollars a day – that's about one pound, or one euro fifty cents. So I suppose I thought that if I wrote an article like this, it would make people reflect for a moment on the everyday choices that we make. Maybe if we all change the way we live a little, it will give the poor people in the world a chance to have a better standard of living.

Finally, I'd just like to thank all the wonderful people I've met since I've been in the UK – especially Rob, Emily, Steve, Rebecca and Jackie. Thanks to all of you for being so supportive and helping me so much. If it hadn't been for you, I would never have won the competition.

KEY

1 c   2 b   3 b   4 b   5 a

7 Speaking

- Divide students into pairs. Remind them that they have come to the end of the *New Horizons* story and that they have discussed the different people at many stages throughout.
- At this stage, ask them to think about the future. Remind them about the different life choices that they have seen in the unit and ask them to think about the different characters in terms of their future decisions.

- Refer them to the names of the characters and to the photo at the bottom of the page to refresh their memories. They discuss each character. Monitor, helping out as necessary.
- When students have finished, get feedback about each character from one or two pairs. Encourage the rest of the class to agree or disagree and to give their own opinions.

8 Writing

- Using some of the ideas they thought about in exercise 7, students choose one of the characters from the story to write about. If possible, try to make sure that each character is chosen at least once.
- Refer them to the different points and remind them to use the vocabulary on page 79. Encourage them to use a range of structures, including a variety of conditional sentences if possible.
- The activity can be set for homework.

Extension
Language plus p.100

Language review pages 84–85

Vocabulary

1
1 b   2 c   3 a   4 a   5 c   6 b   7 a   8 b

2
1 get   2 start   3 buy   4 live   5 stay   6 having
7 getting   8 go

Grammar

3
Possible answers:
1 We used to play in the park when we were children.
2 ✓
3 ✓
4 Did you use to phone her often before you split up?
5 My parents used to get on well with my aunt.
6 ✓
7 I used to play cards when I was young.
8 I'm not really used to getting up early.

4
1 have you tidied   2 'm watching   3 'll do   4 say
5 is going to call   6 are you going   7 're meeting
8 haven't spoken   9 wanted   10 will go   11 's got
12 wants

5

Transcript 2.28
See Student's Book page 84 and Key to exercise 4.

6
Possible answers:
1 I would have come to the party if you had invited me.
2 I would have worn my boots if I had known it was going to snow.
3 I would have passed the exam if I hadn't felt so ill.
4 I would have got up earlier if I hadn't forgotten when she was arriving.
5 I would have ordered Tim a present if I had some money.
6 I would have been at school if I hadn't forgotten my alarm clock.

7
2 Alicia wishes she hadn't gone to Australia.
3 Alicia wishes she hadn't fallen in love with Eric.
4 Alicia wishes she hadn't spent all her money on a big engagement party.
5 Alicia wishes she hadn't come back to the UK too late to start her university course.
6 Alicia wishes she hadn't left the UK.

8
Students' own answers.

Communication

9–10
Students' own answers.

11
1 time 2 mind 3 How 4 a 5 Take 6 an 7 out 8 sort

Extra Practice
CD-ROM

Language plus

Language plus 1

Objectives
To revise and extend the material covered in Unit 1
Vocabulary: Health and fitness
Grammar: *used to*; verbs with *to*-infinitive or *–ing*; comparative adverbs
Reading: Changing lifestyles
Speaking: Comparing abilities
Project work: Profile of a star

Estimated time: 2 hours + time for topic research

I decided to change pages 86–87

Warm-up

- Write *couch potato* on the board. Ask the students if they can guess what it means. Elicit that a couch potato is a term used to describe somebody who spends most of their time sitting down (playing computer games, watching TV, etc.).

- Allow students two minutes to think of the disadvantages of being a couch potato. Get some feedback from each pair.

1

- Draw students' attention to the four photos at the top of the page. In pairs, they discuss how each of the photos is related to health and fitness.

- Get feedback from the class.

KEY

Possible answers:

A Fast food is an example of food that is not good for your health.

B Playing computer games is an example of an activity that does not give you much exercise.

C Swimming is good exercise for keeping fit and healthy.

D Fruit and vegetables are necessary to maintain a healthy lifestyle.

2

- Divide students into A/B pairs. Student A reads about Tom and student B reads about Becky. Point out that they don't need to think about the gaps at this stage.

- They match two of the pictures in exercise 1 to their texts. Students compare their answers in pairs. Check answers as a class.

KEY

Tom: B, C

Becky: A, D

3

- Remind students about using *used to* to talk about past habits (page 7) and about using either the *to*-infinitive or the *–ing* form of the verb (page 10). Ask them why they

might use *used to* in these texts and elicit that both Tom and Becky have changed their habits: they no longer do things that they regularly did in the past.

- Students complete the texts with the correct form of the verbs in brackets. When they have finished, students check their answers in pairs.

4

- Play the recording for the students to check their answers to exercise 3.

- In pairs, students decide who they think changed their lifestyle more, Tom or Becky. Get some feedback from each pair.

Transcript 2.29

See Student's Book page 86 and Key.

KEY

1 used to spend
2 didn't use to get
3 to change
4 running
5 to go
6 being
7 didn't use to lead
8 used to be
9 used to eat
10 dieting
11 eating
12 didn't use to be

Students' own answers.

5

- Students read both texts again to decide if the statements are true or false, correcting the false statements.

- Monitor the students as they work, helping out with any problems as necessary.

- When the students are ready, they check their answers in pairs. Check answers as a class.

KEY

1 F: Tom is very keen on keeping fit.
2 T.
3 F: Tom didn't have many friends because he played his games console.
4 T.
5 T.
6 F: Becky used to be quite overweight.
7 T.
8 T.
9 F: She didn't use to be any good in the kitchen.
10 T.

6

- Remind students about adverb formation (see page 9). Students put the sentences into the correct order.

- Students check their answers in pairs. Check answers as a class.

2 Tom won the swimming competition very easily.
3 You will get there if you walk fast.
4 We must do this exercise quickly.
5 I wrote his address very carefully.
6 He kicked the ball really hard.

7

- Ask students what comparative adverbs are and elicit that they are used to compare how people do things (see page 9). Remind students that there are some irregular comparative adverbs.

- Students complete the sentences using comparative adjectives. They check their answers in pairs. Check answers as a class.

2 I speak English more fluently than you.
3 We work harder than you.
4 Jane talks more loudly than Mary.
5 Deborah drives faster than Julie.
6 She sings worse than me!

8

- Refer students to the verbs and adverbs in the box. Ask them to think about two people that they know or two famous people.

- Students use six of the verbs and adverbs to make six comparative sentences about the two people they chose.

- Monitor the students as they work, helping out where necessary.

- When students have finished, they compare their sentences with their partners' sentences. Ask a few students to read their sentences for the rest of the class.

Students' own answers.

Communication • Profile of a star page 87

9

- Students work in small groups of three or four. Ask them to agree on a famous person that they admire. Refer them to the questions and encourage them to think of reasons why they admire this person.

- Monitor, helping out with ideas or vocabulary as necessary. Get brief feedback from each group.

10

- Read the task together in class. If this is the first time students are doing a research task in *New Horizons*, it may be a good idea to check, in the students' own language, that they know what they need to do. This will help you refer back to this discussion later in similar tasks.

- Elicit some suggestions for sources of information about the famous person the students have chosen. These may include magazines or, more likely, information websites such as Wikipedia. Make sure students understand the prompts to help them in their research and remind them that they should make notes as they research.

- You may like to set the research stage as homework, to follow up in class in the next lesson. In this case, students can do some research on their method individually, and then combine their information for the next activity.

11

- When students have finished their research, they can make a poster to illustrate the profile of their star. To make a poster, students will need access to paper, coloured pens and somewhere to print some pictures to illustrate their proposal. This could be set for homework, but if set as a class activity, it can be a relaxed and informal setting for practising English.

- Make sure you allocate enough time for the students to prepare their poster. Circulate to help out with ideas and encourage them to speak only in English as they work together.

12

- Students present their famous person to the class. Remind them that they should be talking about how this person changed when they became famous; therefore, they should be using *used to* to talk about what their life was like before they became a celebrity.

- Encourage the other students to make notes on each presentation. When each group has finished, have a class vote on which group presented the best method.

Extension

Individual work: I'm a star!

- Tell students to imagine that they are now famous. Encourage them to create a glamorous lifestyle for themselves. They should think about why they are famous, how they became famous, what they do differently and what they miss about their normal life.

- Students write a description of their rise to fame. Encourage them to use *used to* and different verb forms as they describe how their life changed.

- This activity could be set as homework.

Further practice
CD-ROM Units 1 and 2

Language plus 2

Objectives

To revise and extend the material covered in Unit 2

Vocabulary: The body; appearance; advice

Grammar: *have/get* something *done* ; *should/ought to*

Listening: Getting a tattoo

Project work: Preparing advice for body art

Estimated time: 2 hours + time for topic research

Body image   pages 88–89

Warm-up

- Students work in pairs. Tell them they have to choose between getting a tattoo or getting a piercing. In their pairs, they have two minutes to discuss and decide. Encourage them to think of reasons for their decision.
- Get feedback from each pair. How many students would prefer a tattoo? How many would prefer a piercing? Why?

1

- Draw students' attention to the pictures. In pairs, they briefly discuss what they can see and what the people might be talking about.
- Get some ideas from a few pairs.

2

- Tell students they are going to hear the conversation between the people in the pictures.
- Play the recording. Were the students' predictions in exercise 1 right?

Transcript 2.30

Lara Hey, look! A tattoo shop. Let's go in.
Jake No, thanks. Come on, Andy. Let's have a look in that music shop.
Anisha You don't want a tattoo, surely?
Lara Why not? I want to change my image, and besides, I only want a small tattoo.
Man Hello. What can I do for you?
Lara I'd like to have a tattoo done.
Man Can I see some ID, please?
Lara What for?
Man You have to be 18 to get a tattoo done.
Lara Oh, no! What a drag!
Man Well, why don't you have a henna tattoo done? They aren't permanent and you don't have to be 18. If you walk along the seafront, you'll find people who do them.
Lara OK. Thanks. Bye.
Andy Well, show us your tattoo.
Lara I didn't have a tattoo done. You have to be 18.
Jake Shame! Why don't you get your nose pierced instead?
Andy Or you could get your hair dyed pink.
Lara Very funny. Anyway, I'm going to have a henna tattoo done now.
Anisha Well, let's all go to the seafront, then.

3

- Refer students to the questions and allow them time to read them. Remind them that it is useful to underline key words to help them focus on the recording.
- Play the recording. Students do the task and check their answers in pairs. Check answers as a class.

Transcript 2.30

See exercise 2.

KEY

1 Anisha goes into the tattoo shop with Lara.
2 She wants to change her image.
3 She can't have one done because she isn't 18.
4 He suggests getting a henna tattoo because they are not permanent.
5 They suggest that Lara should get her nose pierced or her hair dyed pink.
6 No, they are joking.

4

- Refer students to the sentences from the recording. Ask them if they can remember who says each sentence.
- They check their answers in pairs. Play the recording one last time to check answers as a class.

Transcript 2.30

See exercise 2.

KEY

1 Anisha   2 Lara   3 Lara   4 Andy   5 Lara   6 Anisha

5

- Ask the students what Lara wanted to have done and elicit the answer Lara wanted to have a tattoo done. Ask them who was going to do it and elicit that the tattoo artist was going to do it. Remind students of the structure and use of *have/get* something *done* (see page 17).
- Students put the sentences from the conversation into the correct order. They check their answers in pairs. Check answers as a class.

KEY

2 You have to be eighteen to get a tattoo done.
3 Why don't you have a henna tattoo done?
4 I didn't have a tattoo done.
5 Why don't you get your nose pierced instead?
6 You could get your hair dyed pink.

6

- Refer students to the words in the box and ask them what they are often used for. Elicit that they are often used for giving advice (see page 19).
- Students imagine that they are Lara's parents and that they are giving her advice. They complete the sentences with the correct words.
- They check their answers in pairs. Check answers as a class.

KEY

1 shouldn't   2 ought   3 were   4 don't   5 better
6 should

7

- Tell students to read the different situations and to write down a piece of advice for each one. Encourage them to use different phrases from page 19 to make their advice sound more natural.
- Monitor the students as they make their sentences. Make sure they are using the structures correctly.

KEY

Students' own answers.

8

- In pairs, students compare the advice they gave for each situation in exercise 7. For each situation, they choose the piece of advice they think is better.
- Get some feedback from a few pairs. Which pair gave the best advice?

Communication • Agony Aunts and Agony Uncles page 89

9

- Students work in small groups of three or four. Ask them to discuss the different types of body art mentioned in exercise 1 and if they would ever consider having any of them done.
- Monitor the students as they speak, helping out where necessary and making a note of any errors to be addressed at a later date.
- Get some feedback from each group.

10

- Students work in their groups and choose one of the types of body art from exercise 9. If possible, make sure that each of the types of body art is chosen at least once.
- Students do some research to find more information about their type of body art. Read through the prompts with them and explain that they are there to give them ideas.
- You may like to set the research stage as homework, to follow up in class in the next lesson. In this case, students can do some research on their method individually, and then combine their information for the next activity.

11

- When each group has combined their information on their body art, separate them and divide students into new groups. The new groups should consist of students who have researched different arts.
- In the new groups, students compare their body arts and discuss the information that they found.

12

- Ask the class if they know what an Agony Aunt or Uncle is? Elicit that it is a person who gives advice in a problem page, normally in magazines.
- Tell the students that each group is going to prepare advice for Lara. They should use the information they have found to tell her what type of body art she should or shouldn't have, or what she should do instead. Encourage students to make notes on their advice.

13

- Each group presents their advice to Lara to the rest of the class. Encourage the other students to make notes as they listen to each group. Have a class vote on which group gave the most helpful advice.

Extension

Individual writing: advice

- Tell students to imagine that they are writing an entry for a teenage magazine's problem page. They have to write about body art and whether they would recommend it or not.
- Encourage students to use the vocabulary from the unit and different ways of giving advice in their entry. The activity could be set for homework.

Further practice
CD-ROM Units 1 and 2

Language plus 3

Objectives

To revise and extend the material covered in Unit 3

Vocabulary: Feelings and emotions

Grammar: Second conditional; *wish* + Past simple; *make* + object + adjective/verb

Reading: Phobias

Speaking: Making wishes

Estimated time: 2 hours

I wish I weren't afraid! pages 90–91

Warm-up

- Tell the students one thing that makes you feel scared, for example, *I really don't like the dark. Being in a dark room makes me very scared.*
- In pairs, students tell each other one thing that makes them feel scared. Get some feedback from a few pairs.

1

- Draw students' attention to the three photos at the top of the page. In pairs, they discuss what each of the people is afraid of.
- Get feedback from the class and put their ideas on the board.

2

- Refer students to the three texts and ask them to read through them quickly to match each one with a photo in exercise 1. Tell them to ignore the gaps for the moment.
- They briefly check answers in pairs.

KEY

Justin C   Erica A   Keith B

3

- Ask the students what the Second conditional is used for and elicit that we use it to talk about an imaginary situation or something that is very unlikely to happen. Elicit the structure of the Second conditional and put it on the board (see Student's Book page 27).
- Students complete the texts with the correct forms of the verbs in brackets. They check their answers in pairs. Check answers as a class.

KEY

1 lived   2 'd never go out   3 had to   4 'd choose
5 had to   6 wouldn't be   7 'd be   8 saw   9 was
10 I'd leave   11 would I do   12 lived

4

- Play the recording for students to check their answers in exercise 3.

Transcript 🎧 2.31

See Student's Book page 90 and Key.

Extension

Pairwork: Conditional chain

- Remind students about the story they made using the second conditional in exercise 4 on page 27.
- Write the following sentence on the board: *If I were afraid of open spaces, I'd never leave the house.* Working in pairs, students continue the chain with their own ideas. Ask them to create five more sentences, reminding them that the second clause of each sentence will become the first clause of the next sentence. Monitor, helping as necessary.
- When students are finished, ask each pair to read out their chain. Have a vote on the best/funniest/most original chain.

5

- In pairs, students discuss whether they think the people in exercise 1 are happy or not. Ask them to suggest how they might like their lives to be.
- Get feedback from a few pairs.

KEY

Students' own answers.

6

- Draw students' attention to the incomplete sentences and elicit that we use *wish* to talk about what we would like to be different. Ask them if the Past simple after *wish* refers to the past or the present. Elicit that it refers to the present (see page 29).
- Students complete the sentences and check their answers in pairs. Check answers as a class.

KEY

1 wasn't/weren't   2 liked   3 didn't mind   4 felt
5 had   6 didn't feel

7

- Remind the students about the structure of *make* + object + verb/adjective (see page 30). Point out that the students have two tasks to do. They have to rewrite the sentences using *make*, and then write a sentence using *wish* to imagine the situation was different.
- Students complete the sentences and the wishes. They check their answers in pairs. Check answers as a class.

KEY

Possible answers:

2 … make me nervous. I wish I didn't have one tomorrow.
3 … makes him depressed. He wishes it wasn't raining.
4 … makes me happy. I wish I were in love.
5 … make her impatient. She wishes she weren't in one now.
6 … make me cry. I wish this were a happy movie.
7 … don't make me laugh. I wish you told better ones.
8 … make me bored. I wish I liked them.

8

- Refer students to the list of things that often make people feel afraid. Read through them to check for understanding.
- Students identify which of the items make them afraid. When they are ready, they work in pairs by asking each

other questions about each item. Refer them to the example and remind them to use the correct tenses when using the Second conditional and *wish*.

- Monitor, listening out for correct structures. Make a note of any errors to come back to at a later date.

KEY
Students' own answers.

Communication • A magic lamp page 91

9

- Students work in small groups of three or four. Ask them if they ever heard of the story of *Aladdin* and elicit any information they have about it.
- Tell each group that they can have three wishes. Refer them to the prompts and ask them to discuss what they would like to be different about their lives. Monitor, helping out as necessary but try not to interrupt too much.
- Put any new vocabulary that come up on the board for the whole class to see.

> **CULTURE NOTE** *Aladdin* is a well-known story from the collection of tales called *Arabian Nights* that is based in the Middle East. The main character, Aladdin, finds a magic lamp. When he rubs the lamp, a genie (a spirit with magical powers) appears and offers him three wishes.

10

- Tell students to choose three wishes to ask from their magic lamp. Point out that they should agree on their wishes, as they have to share them. Therefore, they all need to wish the same thing!
- Monitor and make sure they are forming their wishes correctly.

11

- Once each group has finished with their wishes, ask them to make notes on how their life would be different if their wishes came true.
- Point out that they should use the Second conditional as they speak, as they are talking about an imaginary situation. Monitor, helping out as necessary.

12

- Each group presents their wishes to the rest of the class. Encourage the other students to make notes as they listen.
- Have a vote for which group had the best wishes.

> ## Extension
> ### Individual work: I wish I were better at English…
> - Tell students to choose one of the wishes that their group made and to think about how it would make their life better if it were true.
> - Students write a paragraph describing their wish. This can be set for homework.

Further practice
CD-ROM Units 3 and 4

Language plus 4

Objectives

To revise and extend the material covered in Unit 4

Vocabulary: Love and relationships

Grammar: Past perfect; reported speech

Listening: Story of a relationship

Project work: Talking about famous couples

Estimated time: 2 hours + time for topic research

Love hurts   pages 92–93

Warm-up

- Draw students' attention to the title of the lesson, *Love hurts*. Discuss its meaning with them as a class. Do they agree with it? Does anybody disagree?
- Get feedback from a few students, encouraging them to explain their answers.

1

- Draw students' attention to the photos. In pairs, they briefly discuss what they can see and how the people might be feeling. They choose adjectives to describe them.
- Get some feedback from a few pairs.

KEY

Possible answers:

main picture: happy, content, relaxed
small picture: confused, upset, angry, sad

2

- Refer students to the text and ask them to read it quickly to identify which of the photos from exercise 1 suits it best. They check their answers in pairs.
- Check answers as a class.

KEY

The smaller picture of the unhappy couple matches it best.

3

- Draw students' attention to the incomplete paragraph and ask them to compare it with the text in exercise 2. Elicit that it is telling the same story, but that the events are in a different order. Remind students that we can mix up the order of a story to make it more interesting, but we must be careful about what tenses we use.
- Explain that students need to use the Past perfect and Past simple to complete the text. Refer them to page 39 to remind them of the structure of the Past perfect if necessary. Students complete the text and compare their answers in pairs. Check answers as a class.

KEY

1 split up   2 had lied   3 had cheated   4 was
5 had had   6 had fallen   7 tried   8 had had

4

- Refer students to the highlighted sentences in the text in exercise 2. Ask them to translate the phrases into their own language.
- They check their translations in pairs. Then check the translations together as a class.

KEY

Students' own translations.

5

- Tell students they are going to listen to another story about a different couple. Play the recording and ask them if it is similar to or different from that of Jonathan and Sandra.
- Check answers as a class.

Transcript ☺ 2.32

Just before she went on holidays, Chloe split up with her boyfriend, James. She was still in love with him, but she found out that he was cheating on her with someone else at the same time as her. She was very upset because she had a good relationship with him and she enjoyed going out with him. But when she found out about Rachel, they had a terrible row. She told him that she couldn't go out with someone who lied to her. James phoned her several times to try and make up with her. He said that he loved her and that they had lots in common. He said he wanted to get engaged to her and maybe even marry her in the future. He said that he would always tell the truth from then on. She told him to tell that to his new girlfriend and put the phone down.

KEY

It is similar to Jonathan and Sandra's story.

6

- Refer students to the incomplete sentences. Elicit that they need to be completed using reported speech. Remind them that reported speech uses the past form of the verb tense that was used in direct speech (see page 40).
- Students complete the sentences based on the story they just heard. Play the recording a second time for them to check their answers.

KEY

1 couldn't…lied   2 loved…had   3 wanted   4 would (always) tell   5 to tell

7

- Tell students to use the reported speech sentences from exercise 6 to create the sentences as they had been in direct speech. Point out that they have to do the process backwards, and refer them to the table on page 40 to help them.
- Monitor the students as they make their sentences, making sure they are using the structures correctly. Check answers as a class.

KEY

2 'I love you and we have lots in common.'
3 'I want to get engaged to you.'
4 'I'll (always) tell the truth from now on.'
5 'Tell that to your new girlfriend.'

8

- In pairs, students discuss what they would do if they were Sandra or Chloe. Encourage them to use the vocabulary from exercise 4 as they speak. Remind them that they should be using the Second conditional, as they are talking about an imaginary situation (see Unit 3).
- Get some feedback from a few pairs.

Communication • Famous love page 93

9

- Students work in small groups of three or four. Ask them to discuss the photos and to identify the couples in them if they can, saying which of them are real and which of them are fictional. Get feedback from a few groups.
- Draw their attention to the question and they discuss whether they think they are all examples of true love. Encourage them to explain their answers.
- Monitor, helping out as necessary.

KEY

Clockwise from top left:
Romeo and Juliet (fictional), The Duke and Duchess of Cambridge (real), Jack and Rose from the film *Titanic* (fictional), David and Victoria Beckham (real).
Students' own answers.

> **CULTURE NOTE** **Romeo and Juliet** are the main characters in a play by William Shakespeare, which has been adapted many times for stage, television and the cinema. The photo in the exercise is taken from Franco Zeffirelli's film adaptation. **Jack and Rose** are fictional people from James Cameron's film *Titanic* – no passengers of these names travelled on the ill-fated 1912 maiden voyage of the famous cruise liner *Titanic*. Prince William married Katharine Middleton in 2011, and they assumed the titles **The Duke and Duchess of Cambridge**. Footballer **David Beckham** married **Victoria** Adams, a former member of the pop group Spice Girls and to date they have had four children together.

10

- Students work in their groups and choose one of the couples from exercise 9. If possible, try to make sure that each of the couples is chosen by at least one group.
- Draw their attention to the prompts and read through them with the class. Tell them to do some research on their chosen couple and to use the prompts to help them with ideas. (You can find some basic information about the couples in the Culture note above.)
- This stage of the activity could be set for homework, to be followed up in a later class.

11

- Students combine their information on the couple they have chosen in their groups and write a story to explain how they fell in love and what their relationship is like.
- Encourage them to use the Past perfect in their description of their couple's relationship. Monitor the students as they work, helping out with vocabulary and ideas as necessary.

- When they are ready, divide the students into pairs. Each pair should consist of two members from different groups.
- In their pairs, students tell each other the story of the couple they did their research on. Monitor, listening out for correct use of vocabulary and correct use of the Present perfect.

Further practice
CD-ROM Units 3 and 4

Language plus 5

Objectives
To revise and extend the material covered in Unit 5
Vocabulary: Crime and punishment
Grammar: *should have, ought to have, shouldn't have*
Listening: A stolen mobile phone
Speaking: Punishments for crimes
Project work: Proposing solutions to crimes

Estimated time: 2 hours + time for topic research

You shouldn't have done that! pages 94–95

Warm-up

- Tell the students about something you did that was silly and that you regret. For example, *Last week I went shopping. I was in a hurry and I forgot to close the front door to my house. It was very stupid – I was lucky that nobody broke into the house and stole anything.*

- Ask the students to tell you some advice in the past and elicit the sentence *You shouldn't have left the door open.*

- In pairs, students think of something they did that was silly and that they regret. Their partner has to tell them a sentence with *should have* or *shouldn't have*. Get some feedback from each pair.

1

- Draw students' attention to the photo and discuss it with them briefly, talking about the people in it and where they are. Elicit that it looks like something is wrong.

- Allow students time to read the sentences and explain the task. Play the recording. Students put the sentences into the correct order and check their answers in pairs. Play the recording a second time to check answers as a class.

Transcript 2.33

See Students' Book page 94 and Key to exercise 2.

KEY

1 e 2 b 3 f 4 a 5 d 6 c

2

- Refer students to the incomplete dialogue and ask them to try to complete it from memory. They check their answers in pairs.

- Play the dialogue to check answers as a class.

KEY

ought to have gone, shouldn't have put, should have been

3

- Students read the dialogue again and decide if the sentences are true or false. They check their answers in pairs. Check answers as a class.

- Ask the students how they would feel if they were Emma. Put their suggestions on the board.

KEY

1 F: They travelled by coach.
2 F: David says he'll get a table.
3 T.

4 T.
5 F: He thinks they should report it to the police.
6 T.

4

- Remind students about giving somebody past advice and elicit the structures for *should/shouldn't have* and *ought to have*. If necessary, refer them to page 47 to refresh their memories.

- Point out the prompts for sentences and ask them to complete them to make full sentences using *should have, shouldn't have* or *ought to have*.

- They check their answers in pairs. Check answers as a class.

KEY

2 You shouldn't have phoned me so late last night.
3 You ought to have visited the cathedral.
4 He shouldn't have spent all his money.
5 I should have parked my car in the garage.
6 They should have taken an earlier train.
7 You shouldn't have bought such a big present.
8 We ought to have gone to the police.

Extension

Pair work: I should have gone to bed earlier last night…

- Prepare some sentences to read out to the students. Each of them should result in some past advice. For example, *I'm feeling very tired today; I didn't have enough time to finish my homework; There is a lot of litter on the street*, etc.

- Read out each sentence to the class. They write down a response to each one using *should/shouldn't have* or *ought to have*. When you have finished, they compare their sentences in pairs.

- Get some feedback from each pair.

5

- Refer students to the situations and explain that they need to respond to each one with some past advice. Read the example with them. They do the task individually.

- Students compare their sentences in pairs. Check answers as a class.

KEY

Possible answers:
2 She should have gone to the dentist earlier.
3 They should have taken the bus.
4 He shouldn't have eaten so much.
5 I should have brought a book with me.
6 She shouldn't have spent all her money.

6

- Refer students to the crimes in the box. Ask them to try to translate them from memory. If they need to, they can refer to page 47 to help them.

- Students compare their translations with each other. Check them as a class.

KEY

Students' own translations.

7

- Remind students that each of the crimes in exercise 6 has a criminal that commits it. In pairs, they write down the criminal for each crime in a sentence that also contains the verb.
- Check answers as a class.

KEY

The person who burgles is a burglar.
The person who mugs is a mugger.
The person who vandalises is a vandal.
The person who shoplifts is a shoplifter.
The person who pickpockets is a pickpocket.

8

- Working in pairs, students rank the crimes in exercise 6 from the most serious to the least serious. Encourage them to discuss each crime and to justify their rankings.
- Monitor, helping out as necessary. Get feedback from each pair. Do all of the students agree with each other?

KEY

Students' own answers.

Communication • Crimebusters! page 95

9

- Read the instructions with the class and make sure they understand what they have to do.
- Divide the class into small groups of three or four. Ask them to look at the prompts and to organise their research. In other words, they should allocate different crimes to different people in the group to make their research more efficient.
- The research stage is probably best to be done for homework, but make sure that everybody knows what piece of research they are responsible for.
- When the research stage is complete, students work in their groups and combine their information. Encourage them to tell each other about what they found and how they think their crimes might be best punished.
- Monitor, helping out as necessary. Make a note of any errors you would like to come back to at a later time.
- Encourage students to prepare short presentations for their ideas to the rest of the class.

10

- Each group presents their ideas from exercise 9 to the rest of the class. Encourage the other students to make notes as they listen.
- Have a vote on the best proposals for reducing each crime.

Extension

Individual writing: crime and punishment

Ask each student to choose one of the crimes that they researched and write a short paragraph that describes the crime and how they think it should be punished.

▌Further practice
▌CD-ROM Units 5 and 6

Language plus 6

Objectives

To revise and extend the material covered in Unit 6

Vocabulary: World problems

Grammar: Passive forms

Reading: Newspaper articles

Project work: Charity research

Estimated time: 2 hours + time for topic research

Social ills `pages 96–97`

Warm-up

- Draw students' attention to the title of the lesson, *Social ills*. Ask them what *ill* means and elicit that it normally means somebody is not feeling very well. Ask them what they think social ills means and elicit that it refers to problems in society.

1

- Draw students' attention to the photos. In pairs, they briefly discuss what they can see.
- Students match the photos to the social problems. They check their answers in pairs. Check answers as a class.

KEY

1 B   2 A   3 C   4 D   5 E   6 F

2

- Refer students to the vocabulary in the box and explain that each of the social problems in exercise 1 matches with a word for each of the three columns in the table.
- In pairs, students complete the table. Check their answers as a class.

KEY

Adjectives:

1 poor   2 addicted   3 drunk   4 violent
6 unemployed

Expressions with verbs:

1 beg   2 take drugs   3 drink   4 mug   5 sleep rough

People:

2 a drug addict   3 an alcoholic   4 a mugger
5 a homeless person   6 an unemployed person

3

- Draw students' attention to the incomplete news articles. Ask them to skim-read each of them, ignoring the gaps, to find out what each of them is talking about. Article A is talking about statistics for alcoholism in the UK, B is talking about people getting mugged for their phones and C is talking about educating people about homelessness.
- Students complete the gaps with vocabulary from exercise 2. They check their answers in pairs. Check answers as a class.

KEY

1 alcoholism   2 addiction   3 alcoholic   4 violent
5 mugger   6 homeless   7 sleeping rough

4

- Refer students to the underlined verbs in the articles. Ask them to identify which tenses they are using and what they are called. Refer them to pages 57 and 59 if necessary.
- They check answers in pairs. Check answers as a class.

KEY

was discovered: Past simple passive
are stolen: Present simple passive
have been consulted: Present perfect passive
will be prevented: Future passive

5

- Refer students to the incomplete sentences and ask them to complete them using the correct form of the passive.
- Remind them to think carefully about the tense that they will need to complete each sentence. They check their answers in pairs. Check answers as a class.

KEY

1 is being painted   2 was sent   3 has been closed
4 will be built   5 haven't been told   6 were chosen
7 has never been won   8 is being held

6

- Draw students' attention to the sentences and elicit that they are all active. Point out that they would be better in the passive form because we don't know who is doing the action in many of the situations (*they* or *someone*).
- Students rewrite the sentences in the passive form. They check their answers in pairs. Check answers as a class.

KEY

1 … will be checked at the airport.
2 … has been stolen.
3 … is being questioned by the police.
4 … won't be met at the station.
5 … is being opened by the Minister.
6 … have been sent out.

Communication • A helping hand `page 97`

7

- Divide students into small groups of three or four. Refer them back to the social problems in exercise 1. In their groups, they have to decide which of them is the most serious problem and which of them is the least serious problem.
- Encourage them to think about the effects of each problem on both the people and on society as well. Monitor, helping out with ideas and vocabulary as necessary.
- Get some feedback from each group about their opinions. Encourage a class discussion on the topic. Try not to interrupt the students and make a quiet note of any error that you would like to address later.

8

- Students work in their groups. Read the instructions for the task with the students and make sure they know what they have to do.
- Ask each group to choose a problem to research. If they like, they can each focus on one of the prompts as

they research, or they can focus on different points and combine their information afterwards.

- The research stage can be done for homework, to be followed up in a later class.

9

- Students work in their groups and combine the information they found. Encourage them to prepare a short presentation on their charity and make sure they remember to talk about each of the different points.

- Students present their charities to the class. Encourage the other students to make notes and ask questions about the charities they hear about.

Extension

Individual writing: newspaper article

Ask each student to write a short article about the social problem and the charity they focused on in exercises 7 and 8. Encourage them to use the vocabulary they learned in Unit 6 and to try to use the passive form where possible.

Further practice
CD-ROM Units 5 and 6

Language plus 7

Objectives
To revise and extend the material covered in Unit 7
Vocabulary: Technology
Grammar: Phrasal verbs; *be/get used to*
Listening: Favourite gadgets
Speaking: Comparing gadgets

Estimated time: 2 hours

I'm not used to gadgets pages 98–99

Warm-up

- Write *gadgets* on the board and ask the class if they know what it means. Elicit that a gadget is a technological device.

- Have a brainstorming activity with the class. Allow them two minutes to shout out different gadgets. Put their suggestions on the board to ensure correct spelling and pronunciation. If necessary, model and drill the pronunciation of any words that may be problematic – especially those that are pronounced differently in the students' language.

1

- Draw students' attention to the pictures of the four gadgets on page 98. In pairs, they discuss each gadget. Encourage them to briefly think about the usefulness of each one and to talk about whether they have anything similar themselves.

- Monitor, helping out as necessary. Get some feedback from a few pairs.

2

- Tell the students that they are going to listen to three people talking about their favourite gadgets. Draw their attention to the names and explain the task.

- Play the recording. Student match each speaker with a device from exercise 1. Check answers as a class.

Transcript 2.34

Martina I don't know how I'd live without it! It wakes me up in the morning and I have it with me all day long. I do everything on it: I listen to music, I play games and I keep in touch with my friends. It's so much better than the older type of phones. I could never go back to one of them!

Peter I got it as a present from my uncle last Christmas. It was very generous of him, but we do get on with each other very well and he always gives me great presents. I love it! It's quite small so it fits easily into my bag. I do a lot of my schoolwork on it and I also use it to store my photos and music collection, as well as surf the Internet of course. What I like best is that it's so fast. I can't put up with slow computers anymore!

Jenny I wanted one of them for a long time and I asked my parents to get one for me. They said that I had to grow up a bit because I'm quite careless with things like phones and cameras. But they finally gave me one for my birthday and now I just can't put it down! It's so great to be able to

carry so many books around on one small gadget. I just love reading and I'll take very good care of this device.

KEY
Martina 2 (smartphone)   **Peter** 1 (laptop)
Jenny 4 (eReader)

3

- Refer students to the incomplete sentences and point out that they were all used in the recording. Encourage them to work through them individually to try to complete them using phrasal verbs. They check their answers in pairs.

- Play the recording so they can check their answers. Check answers as a class.

KEY
1 wakes…up   2 go back   3 get on with   4 put up with   5 grow up   6 put it down

4

- Point out the verbs on the left and the particles on the right and ask students to match them to make phrasal verbs.

- Check answers as a class. Students then make a sentence for each phrasal verb to illustrate their meaning. Monitor to ensure that they are using the phrasal verbs in the right way. If necessary, remind them of the different types (see Student's Book page 67). They compare their sentences in pairs.

KEY
Possible combinations:
2 f 3 e 4 a 5 b 6 c
Students' own answers.

5

- Refer students to the text and ask them to skim-read it quickly ignoring the gaps for the moment to find out what Norah's opinion on technology is. Elicit that it is generally positive, although she doesn't use or understand the devices herself.

- Ask students to briefly discuss in pairs what their own parents and grandparents or older relatives think about new technological devices. Get some feedback from each pair.

6

- Ask students to complete the paragraph with the correct form of the verbs in brackets. Remind them to think about whether Norah is talking about past habits or about whether or not she is familiar with something (*be used to*; see page 70).

KEY
1 call   2 contacting   3 texting

7

- Ask students what the difference between *be used to* and *get used to* (see page 70) is. Elicit that *be used to* refers to the state of being familiar with something while *get used to* refers to the process of becoming familiar with something.

- Explain the task to the class. Working individually, they write six sentences and use each form three times.

Monitor to make sure they are using the structure correctly and to imply the correct meaning.

KEY
Students' own answers.

8

- Students compare their sentences from exercise 7. Encourage them to look for things in common as well as to look for any differences. Monitor, helping out where necessary and listening for correct use of *be/get used to*.

- Get some feedback from each pair by asking them to describe what they are both used to or what different things they are used to.

Communication • A simple life page 99

9

- Read the task with the class and point out the gadgets in the box. Divide the students into small groups.

- They start discussing the different gadgets. Monitor, making sure they are following the instructions and talking about how important each one is and whether they are used to using it or not.

- Help out with ideas or vocabulary as necessary. Put any new vocabulary on the board for the whole class to use.

- Get some feedback from each pair.

10

- In their groups, students decide which one device they would not be able to live without. Encourage them to think of reasons to support their opinion.

- Monitor, helping out where necessary.

11

- Read the instructions and prompts with the class. In their groups, they discuss how their lives would be different without their chosen device.

- Encourage them to make some notes for each point. Monitor, helping out where you can but try not to interrupt the students too much as they are speaking. Make a note of any general errors you want to come back to later.

12

- If time permits, students make a poster to illustrate what their life would be like without their chosen device.

Extension

Individual work: I couldn't live without it!

- Tell students to write a short essay to describe a simple life with no devices. They can choose to focus on the device they chose in exercise 10, or they can choose a different device if they would like to.

- Encourage them to plan their writing by making brief notes and putting them into a logical order. Remind them to check their writing for mistakes they may have made.

- This activity could be set as homework.

Further practice
CD-ROM Units 7 and 8

Language plus 8

Objectives

To revise and extend the material covered in Unit 8

Vocabulary: Life choices

Grammar: *wish* + Past perfect; Third conditional

Listening: University regrets

Speaking: Imagining the past

Estimated time: 2 hours + time for topic research

I wish I had done it differently   pages 100–101

Warm-up

- Write *university* on the board and ask the class to discuss what they think life at university is like. Elicit ideas from the students and make notes on the board.

- Ask students to group the experiences mentioned into positive and negative experiences.

1

- Draw students' attention to the four photos on the page. Explain that they are all related to university life.

- Refer them to the bullet points and ask them to use them to describe each photo. In pairs, students describe the photos to each other. Ask them to think about their own feelings towards the situations shown.

- Monitor, helping out where necessary. When students have finished, choose a few pairs to describe different photos for the rest of the class.

- Round off the activity by discussing with the class whether they would like to go to university or not.

2

- Tell the class that they are going to listen to Daniel talking about university.

- Play the recording. Students answer the question and check their answers in pairs. Check the answer as a class.

Transcript 🔊 2.35

Daniel I really wish I had studied harder at school. I didn't pass my final exams because I wanted to have fun with my friends instead of studying. So, I had my fun but because I failed my exams, I wasn't able to begin university last month. My best friend, Liam, started university and he is really enjoying himself. I feel so stupid and I wish I had been more sensible. If I had just studied for one hour every morning, I would have got much better results. I would have got a place on the course that I wanted and I would have left home. I would have found a house to share with Liam. But, instead, I have to repeat the year. I really don't like being back with students who are one year younger than me! However, I've learned my lesson and I'm going to work very hard this year. I just wish that somebody had invented time travel so that I could go back to the past and change everything!

KEY
He didn't get into university because he didn't work hard enough.

3

- Ask the students if they think that Daniel would like to change the past and elicit that he probably would.

- Draw their attention to the incomplete sentences and ask the class what kind of sentences they are. Elicit that they are regrets and that they are using the *wish* + Past perfect structure and the Third conditional. Refer students to pages 77 and 80 if necessary.

- Play the recording again. Students complete the sentences using the correct form of the verbs in brackets. Check answers as a class.

Transcript 🔊 2.35
See exercise 2.

KEY
1 had studied   2 had been   3 had just studied
4 would have got   5 would have left
6 would have found   7 had invented

4

- Explain that the sentences in exercise 3 are Daniel's regrets. They describe what he would like to have been different.

- Students write what actually happened to Daniel in each situation. Refer them to the example and compare it to the first sentence.

- Students check their answers in pairs. Check answers as a class.

KEY
2 He wasn't sensible.
3 He didn't study for one hour every evening and he didn't get good results.
4 He didn't get a place on the course that he wanted.
5 He didn't leave home.
6 He didn't find a house to share with Liam.
7 Nobody has invented time travel.

5

- Students match the sentence halves together to form correct sentences. When they have finished, ask them to identify what kind of conditional each sentence is.

- They check answers in pairs. Check answers as a class.

KEY
1 g (Third)   2 d (First)   3 h (First)   4 a (Second)
5 b (Third)   6 f (Third)   7 e (Second)   8 c (Second)

6

- Ask students to think about their past and to think of five things they would like to have done differently.

- They make five sentences to illustrate their ideas. Encourage them to use a combination of the Third conditional and *wish* + Past perfect in their sentences.

- Monitor the activity to make sure they are using the structures correctly.

7

- Working in pairs, students compare their sentences. Ask them to identify any similar regrets that they have.

- For each regret, ask students to give each other advice. They cannot change the past, but perhaps they can do something about the future. For example, *I wish I had studied harder for last week's exam. Well, you should study harder for the next one.*
- Monitor the students as they speak, making a note of any errors you would like to come back to later.

Communication • An imaginary past page 101

8

- Read the first part of the task with the students. Divide them into pairs and ask them to imagine life 100 years ago. They think about how it would have been different. Encourage them to make some notes as they speak.
- Get some feedback from each pair, pointing out that they should be using Third conditional forms as they speak.
- Refer students to the research part of the task. Draw their attention to the different points. Encourage them to try to find out more information about life 100 years ago. They could do their research on the Internet, or for a more personal approach, they could find out about life from an older relative who would know more.
- Point out that they should make notes as they do their research so that they can combine them when they are next in class.

9

- In their pairs, students combine their notes and use them to create their posters. Point out that they can use their imagination if they like: they were not alive then, so they have to imagine what would have happened.
- Help out with ideas as necessary.

10

- Students present their posters to the class in their pairs. Remind them that they are talking about what would have happened so they have to use the Third conditional as they speak.
- The rest of the class should make notes and ask relevant questions where appropriate.
- When all of the presentations are finished, have a vote on the most interesting past.

Extension

Individual work: I would have been…

- Tell students to write a short essay to describe their imaginary past. If they like they can use the information from exercises 8 and 9, or they can choose another period that they would like to have lived in.
- Point out that they must use the Third conditional, as it is an imaginary situation in the past. The activity can be set for homework.

Further practice
CD-ROM Units 7 and 8

Workbook Answer Key

Unit 1

1

Across
1 weights
3 gym
5 aerobics
6 pitch
11 rowing
13 unfit
14 kick boxing
Down
2 gymnastics
4 pool
7 court
8 karate
9 Tai Chi
10 yoga
12 judo

2
1 does
2 went
3 playing
4 do
5 does
6 played

3
1 My grandfather used to read a lot when he could see better.
2 Did you use to go skiing when you lived in Slovenia?
3 My aunt used to be thinner when she was younger.
4 We didn't use to go to the mountains on holiday when we were children.
5 She used to buy a new dress every month.
6 Did you use to get up early when you were a child?
7 I used to go to the cinema twice a week.
8 They used to live in the country. They used to have a farm.

4
1 used to have
2 didn't use to have
3 used to walk
4 used to take
5 used to be
6 used to play
7 used to sit
8 used to like
9 used to read
10 used to hate
questions:
2 Did Heather use to catch the bus home? No, she didn't.
3 Did Heather use to play with Jane? Yes, she did.
4 Did Heather use to like running? No, she didn't.
5 Did Heather use to do yoga? No, she didn't.

5
Possible answers:
1 She used to be a nurse. She didn't use to be a farmer.
2 He used to be a bad student. He didn't use to be good at Grammar. He didn't use to be good at Maths.
3 She used to live in Norway. She didn't use to live in England. She didn't use to live in Spain.
4 You used to sleep well as a baby. You used to smile as a baby. You didn't use to cry a lot as a baby.
5 My grandparents used to play tennis. My grandparents didn't use to play basketball. My grandparents didn't use to play cards.
6 We didn't use to have a dog. We didn't use to have a cat. We didn't use to have a turtle.

6
1 usually
2 crazily
3 late/lately
4 really
5 possibly
6 magically
7 dangerously
8 easily
9 terribly
10 happily

7
good   well   better
far   far   further
hard   hard   harder
careful   carefully   more carefully
slow   slowly   more slowly
bad   badly   worse
quick   quickly   more quickly

8
2 more quickly
3 more easily
4 more carefully
5 more slowly
6 better
7 harder
8 worse

9
1 Nick plays basketball better than James.
2 Martin runs faster than Jake.
3 My mum drives more safely than my dad.
4 John learns more easily than his brother.
5 He works more slowly than his colleague.
6 Jackie sings more beautifully than me.

10
Students' own translations:
1 Tanya runs faster than Nicole.
2 Yesterday Oxford United played much better than Swindon Town.
3 Paul doesn't play football as well as Andy.

4 You can contact him more quickly by email.
5 In cities bikes often travel faster than cars.
6 After the accident Sonia started to drive more carefully.

11
1 to eat
2 smoking
3 to learn
4 to give me back
5 'd like to go
6 to buy
7 doing
8 to be

12
1 forgot to give
2 stopped talking
3 hoping to become
4 tried to call
5 like to go out

13
Students' own answers.

Unit 1 Revision

A
1 Melanie cooks better than Andrea.
2 The team played badly.
3 Did you use to do sport when you were a child?
4 I used to go to the gym twice a week.
5 John drives more carefully than Bob.
6 Keep going, the library is at the end of this street.
7 I'll never forget meeting Orlando Bloom!
8 The teacher suggested doing her course.
(There are no correct sentences.)

B
1 Did you use to
2 did
3 do you
4 well
5 Did you use to
6 didn't
7 did you use to
8 to eat
9 eat
10 eating

C
Students' own translations:
1 I stopped playing football.
2 Anne used to live in Glasgow but now she lives in Birmingham.
3 I hope to go to Italy this summer.
4 When I was a child, I used to like playing football but I don't like it now.
5 I refuse to study on Saturday evening.
6 Did you use to go to the swimming pool every day?
7 Emma plays basketball better than me.
8 They speak French worse than me.

Unit 2

1
Across
4 elbow
6 tooth
8 stomach
11 chin
12 wrist
13 leg
14 thumb
16 eyebrow
18 hair
19 ear
20 lip
23 arm
24 neck
Down
1 toe
2 mouth
3 foot
5 shoulder
7 hand
9 chest
10 finger
15 nail
17 bottom
19 eye
22 nose

2
2 to have your eyes tested.
3 to have your car repaired.
4 to have your photos printed.
5 to have your hair cut.
6 to have your teeth checked.

3
2 How often do you have your teeth checked?
3 Have they had their homework marked yet?
4 Where do you usually have your hair cut?
5 Are we going to have the food delivered?
6 Did they have their/the swimming pool cleaned last week?

4
1 I am going to have my computer repaired.
2 He is going to have a new novel published by the end of the year.
3 I am having my Maths homework checked.
4 He is having a new house built.
5 Martha had her photograph taken yesterday.
6 I'm having my ears pierced tomorrow.
7 Gary will have his tattoo removed.
8 Jenny had her passport renewed last week.

5
2 had your camera repaired
3 had your car fixed
4 had it cleaned
5 had some flowers sent
6 had your hair cut
7 have a pizza delivered
8 have the tickets sent

6
1 should speak/ought to speak
2 should go/ ought to go
3 shouldn't eat
4 should do/ought to do
5 shouldn't go
6 should see/ought to see

7
Possible answers:
1 You should watch DVDs in English.
2 You shouldn't use your own language in English lessons.
3 You should travel to an English-speaking country.
4 You should read English books and magazines.
5 You ought to learn ten new words every day.
6 You ought to find an English-speaking penfriend.
7 You ought to listen to songs in English.
8 You ought to find English sites on the Internet.

8
1 You'd better phone your parents, it's very late.
2 If I were you, I wouldn't drink so much coffee.
3 Why don't you take the bus to school today?
4 You'd better go to bed early tonight.
5 If I were you, I would take a painkiller.
6 Why don't you stay in bed?

9
1 I'd go
2 say
3 Why don't you
4 shouldn't
5 Should
6 I wouldn't

10
Students' own translations:
1 You should study the Present perfect more carefully.
2 You'd better check your emails more often.
3 You shouldn't go to school if you have a temperature.
4 I should visit my grandparents more often.
5 Do you think we shouldn't go out?
6 You'd better not do the exam this month.

11
Possible answers:
2 I've got toothache. You should go to the dentist.
3 I've got stomach ache. If I were you, I would go to see a doctor.
4 I've got a sore throat. Why don't you go to a doctor?
5 I've got a headache. You should take a painkiller.
6 I've got backache. If I were you, I would go to see a doctor.

Units 1–2 Revision

A
1 You should buy that jacket.
2 I am going to have my shoes repaired.
3 You ought to come to the judo club with us.
4 You had better tell the teacher why you are late.
5 If I were you, I wouldn't go out in this cold weather.
6 You shouldn't go out with Anne's boyfriend.
7 We are going to have our television fixed on Tuesday.
8 We are having our house designed by a famous architect.

B
1 had
2 hasn't
3 should
4 better
5 ought
6 were
7 Why
8 shouldn't
9 for
10 to

C
Students' own translations:
1 Have you had your hair dyed?
2 Joe had his watch repaired last week.
3 She hasn't had her hair cut for months.
4 What should I do about my weight?
5 You shouldn't send him so many text messages.
6 If I were you, I'd change my job.
7 I've got a sore throat and a cough.
8 You should go and see a doctor urgently.

Exam skills 1–2
See www.oup.com/elt/teachersclub.

Unit 3

1
Across
1 embarrassed
7 laid-back
8 scared
12 nervous
13 OK
16 depressed
17 angry
18 upset
Down
2 bored
3 relieved
4 envious
5 jealous
6 excited
9 annoyed
10 worried
11 confident
14 happy
15 uneasy

2

1 d 2 b 3 a 4 e 5 f 6 c

phrases:

2 If someone stole my bike, I'd get really angry.
3 If I met a famous film star, I'd be very excited.
4 If I could live in another country, I'd choose Brazil.
5 If I could do any job in the world, I'd become a Grand Prix driver.
6 If I found £1,000 in the street, I'd take it to the police station.

Students' own answers.

3

1 were…would go…would go
2 would you do…saw
3 drove…would be
4 would understand…didn't speak
5 wouldn't go…wasn't
6 would you like…weren't
7 wouldn't mind…had
8 didn't live…wouldn't have

4

Possible answers:

1 If I had more free time, I would do more sport.
2 If it stopped raining, we could go out.
3 If you could speak foreign languages, you would get a better job.
4 If people used bikes more, there would be less pollution.
5 You might not love me if I weren't very rich.
6 If I had a digital camera, I could download photos on my computer.

5

Students' own answers.

6

1 d ✓
2 a
3 e ✓
4 b
5 f
6 c ✓

7

Possible answers:

1 I wish I was a bit taller.
2 I wish I could find my mobile.
3 I wish I had a car.
4 I wish I didn't have so much homework.
5 I wish I had straight hair.
6 I wish I lived in Spain.

8

1 I wish I wasn't afraid of dogs.
2 She wishes she was rich.
3 I wish I was taller.
4 He wishes Maths was easier.
5 I wish I didn't have to walk to school.
6 They wish they lived in Rome.
7 I wish I knew the answer.
8 She wishes she could swim.

9

1 Too much homework makes me feel depressed.
2 Funny jokes make me laugh.
3 Going out makes me happy.
4 Travelling makes me feel free.
5 Flying makes me nervous.
6 Spiders make me feel scared.
7 Too many sweets make my brother really excited.
8 Sad films make me cry.

10

Students' own answers.

Units 1–3 Revision

A

Students' own translations:

1 If I were you, I'd try the chocolate cake.
2 If I lost my mobile, my parents wouldn't buy me a new one.
3 I wish I could fly!
4 Driving at night makes me tired.
5 Rebecca wishes she was tall and blonde.
6 If I had more time, I might go to see you.
7 If Tom studied harder, he'd do better at school.
8 People who arrive late make me annoyed.

B

1 passed
2 happy
3 would
4 if
5 to go
6 to go
7 visit
8 'll pass
9 felt
10 nervous
11 shouldn't
12 well

C

Students' own translations:

Ann I wish I lived in the USA.
Richard Why?
Ann Because if I lived in New York, I'd have a more interesting life.
Richard We're very different. I don't like big cities. Going out in big cities makes me feel nervous.
Ann Really? Where would you like to live if you could choose anywhere in the world?
Richard I think I'd choose Sweden.
Ann If you lived in Sweden, you'd have to have lots of money. Life is very expensive in Sweden.
Richard Then maybe I should marry a beautiful, rich Swedish woman!
Ann But would a beautiful, rich Swedish woman want to marry you?
Richard Of course!

Unit 4

1

Across
4 going out
6 cheated on
8 get on
11 made it up
12 row

Down
2 is in love with
3 love
5 get married
7 got engaged
9 put me off
10 lie

2

1
A haven't we?
B aren't you?
2
A aren't you?
B won't you?
3
A did she?
B have they?
4
A wouldn't he?
B does he?
5
A could you?
B haven't you?

3

2 He failed his FCE exam because he hadn't studied enough.
3 They missed the train because they had got up late.
4 We were starving because we hadn't had dinner.
5 He was sick because he had eaten too much.
6 I couldn't get in because I had left my key at home.

4

1 got…had already left
2 arrived…had already started
3 had dinner…had gone
4 phoned…had finished
5 woke up…had had
6 married…had met
7 didn't know…had read
8 was born…had already bought

5

1 had spent
2 flew
3 had…wanted
4 travelled
5 had learnt
6 spoke
7 lived
8 had learnt
9 left

10 continued
11 returned
12 had promised

6

1 had finished
2 started
3 had noticed
4 was
5 had died
6 agreed
7 gave
8 had bought
9 ran
10 had gone

7

1 She told Jane that she was taking an exam that afternoon.
2 My mother said that she'd already had breakfast.
3 Rachel told her parents that she might look for a job for the summer.
4 My friend said that they would go on holiday to Greece.
5 My father said that he was not going to work that day.
6 Bob told me that he was seventeen and lived in Belfast with his family.

8

2 F
that he was going to win the next election.
3 D
that they had won the match the night before very easily.
4 E
that the people of Manchester had just seen an UFO over the city.
5 A
that they would probably make an arrest later that day.
6 B
that they could download his latest album from the Internet.

9

Students' own translations:
1 Joe told me that the red dress really suited me.
2 Martha told me that she had seen Rebecca's new boyfriend.
3 The teacher said we shouldn't bring the dictionary.
4 Susan said that she would arrive at work late.
5 Rob said that he thought he wouldn't come.
6 Nick said that we would bring his CDs.
7 The weather forecast said that it might rain.
8 My mother said that she had already done the washing-up.

10

2 go to Wallace School, don't you?
3 have a brother called Tom, haven't you?
4 are Harry, aren't you?
5 played football with my brother at the weekend, didn't you?
6 didn't win, did you?

Units 1–4 Revision

A

1 I had gone to the shops.
2 she had called me last night, but there had been no answer.
3 We get on very well.
4 Chelsea is going to win!
5 I had packed my bags, I went to the airport.
6 not to go to bed late.

B

Students' own translations:
1 I said to her how nice it was to see her.
2 I asked her what she was doing in London.
3 I said that we had met in Edinburgh the previous summer and asked if she remembered.
4 she said in French, 'I can't speak English.'
5 She also said, 'I've never been to Edinburgh in my life.'
6 I asked her in French, 'What's your name?'
7 she answered, 'My name is Christine.'

C

Students' own translations:
1 You will write to me, won't you?
2 You weren't at the party last night, were you?
3 I had just left the house when my phone rang.
4 When they came out of the cinema, they found they had their car stolen.
5 She told me that I should give up eating junk food.
6 I said that I was a student at the language school but he didn't believe me.
7 She told us she hoped to leave the next day.
8 Jake said he had never seen the film *Mission Impossible*.

Exam skills 3–4

See www.oup.com/elt/teachersclub.

Unit 5

1

1 shoplifting
2 joyriding
3 vandalism
4 drug dealer
5 question
6 arrest
7 pickpocket
8 burglary
9 break into
10 beat up
11 mugger
investigate

2

1 should have/ought to have left
2 should have/ought to have switched
3 should have/ought to have told
4 should have/ought to have walked
5 should have/ought to have come
6 should have/ought to have brought
7 should have/ought to have called
8 should have/ought to have eaten

3

1 Bob shouldn't have/ought not to have driven so fast.
2 My brother shouldn't have/ought not to have gone to school.
3 She shouldn't have/ought not to have drunk so much coffee.
4 I should have/ought to have stayed in my previous job.
5 He shouldn't have/ought not to have worn an expensive watch.
6 She should have/ought to have locked the door.

4

1 He shouldn't have forgotten his umbrella.
2 She ought to have stayed in bed.
3 They should have gone to Jamaica.
4 He shouldn't have stayed at home.
5 They ought to have got to the station earlier.
6 He ought to have stopped at the traffic lights.

5

2 Mike asked Jason where he was from.
3 Mike asked Jason what he was doing in York.
4 Mike asked Jason how long he had been there.
5 Mike asked Jason how long he was going to stay.
6 Mike asked Jason if/whether he was enjoying his course.
7 Mike asked Jason if/whether he had gone to the big rock concert the previous night.
8 Mike asked Jason what time he got home.

6

1 what my phone number was
2 if she would marry him
3 how long the Thames was
4 if I had gone to the cinema the previous night
5 how Tom was
6 if there had been any problems
7 why he was so late
8 if she had phoned him the previous week

7

2 'Can you help me?'
3 'I won't come to the party.'
4 'How long will you stay away?'
5 'Are you going to see him again?'
6 'Don't take too many sweets!'
7 'Buy me a new dress(, please).'
8 'Please give me your phone number.'

8

1 Rebecca's father told her not to go out.
2 Nick's mum wanted him to make his bed in the morning.
3 Robert asked Alice if she wanted to dance.
4 The teacher told the girls to stop talking and to open their books.
5 Jason asked him/her if he/she was enjoying the gig.
6 Mary wanted him/her to lend her his/her scooter.

9

2 her to make some coffee for him
3 Emma to go home before midnight
4 us to open our books
5 Jenny to give him a lift
6 Tom to lend her £20

10

Possible answers:

Ben asked the robber not to shoot him.

The robber said that he didn't want to hurt Ben and asked him to help him to carry the bag.

Ben said that he would do whatever the robber asked him.

The robber wanted Ben to get in the car and drive as fast as possible.

Ben said that he couldn't because there were two police cars in the middle of the road.

The police officer told Big Ron he couldn't escape and ordered him to put the gun down.

The robber asked the police officer not to shoot him.

The police officer told Big Ron that he was arresting him for robbery. And he asked Ben if he was OK.

Ben said that he was fine and that he wanted to go home.

Units 1–5 Revision

A

Students' own translations:

1 You should have asked me to lend you some money.
2 Our neighbour shouldn't have called the police.
3 You should have done the shopping.
4 Sean asked me where Francesca was.
5 We asked them to phone for a taxi.
6 The police officer told the girl to show him her passport.
7 The teacher wanted me to do all the English homework again.
8 He told me to remember to lock the door before going out.

B

1 to talk
2 did they
3 if
4 preferred
5 tell
6 that
7 that
8 was it
9 should
10 would

C

Students' own translations:

Gemma ought to have gone to school today but she didn't feel well. She woke up at seven o'clock and she had a headache and she felt sick. She asked her mother to phone the doctor and he came at nine o'clock. He asked Gemma what she had eaten the previous evening. Gemma told him she hadn't been hungry and she had only eaten an apple. The doctor told her that she shouldn't have eaten so little. He wanted her to have breakfast and to phone him again if she felt sick again.

Unit 6

1

Across

4 collection
7 aid
9 raise
10 homeless
14 poverty
15 refugees
16 diseases
17 sponsor

Down

1 charity
2 famine
3 volunteers
5 orphanage
6 crisis
8 telethon
10 human
11 donate
12 petition
13 starve

2

1 was
2 occurred
3 caused
4 were killed
5 were flooded
6 died
7 was recorded
8 happened
9 was destroyed

3

1 England was invaded by Normans in 1066.
2 America was discovered in 1492.
3 Australia was discovered by Captain Cook in 1770.
4 Queen Victoria was crowned in 1838.
5 Margaret Thatcher was elected Prime Minister in 1979.
6 Princess Diana was killed in a car crash in 1997.

4

1 Meals aren't provided during the flight.
2 Our car can't be repaired.
3 The song will only be performed once.
4 This bridge was built by my grandfather in 1925.
5 Your seat belt must be fastened before taking off.
6 The players are being chosen for tomorrow's football match.
7 This picture was painted by Monet.
8 All the rubbish must be put in the bin.
9 The children were told to speak more quietly.
10 The burglar hasn't been caught by the police yet.

5

1 Who was the ceiling of the Sistine Chapel in Rome painted by?
2 Where should the date be written?
3 How often are they given a test by the teacher?
4 When is breakfast served?
5 How will all the details be sent?
6 Where were my keys found?
7 Who was *The Hobbit* written by?
8 When is the conference being/going to be held?

6

Students' own translations:
In 1886, Coca-Cola was invented by Dr John Pemberton, a chemist from Atlanta, Georgia. The name had been suggested to him by his friend Frank Robinson. At first, the drink could only be bought in one chemist's in Atlanta. Fewer than ten glasses of Coca-Cola were sold a day. By the end of 1890, Coca-Cola was one of America's most popular drinks. In 1985 it was the first fizzy drink to be drunk by astronauts in space. Now more than a billion cans and bottles of Coca-Cola are drunk every day, and it is sold in more than 200 countries all over the world.

7

2 False! Prince Edward wasn't made King of England on 16th May 2007.
3 False! A cure for AIDS hasn't been found.
4 False! It hasn't been decided to make people drive on the right.
5 True.
6 False! Tom Cruise hasn't been married to Madonna.
7 False! The euro hasn't been adopted as the official currency in the UK.
8 False! Hillary Clinton hasn't been elected the first woman President of the USA.

8

1 yourself
2 myself
3 ourselves
4 themselves
5 ourselves
6 herself

9

1 each other
2 each other
3 themselves
4 themselves
5 themselves
6 each other

10

1 myself
2 himself
3 each other
4 itself
5 –
6 each other
7 –
8 –
9 herself
10 himself

11

2 each other
3 himself
4 each other
5 herself
6 myself
7 each other
8 each other

12

2 Where will it be held?
3 When will it be held?
4 Which bands are being booked?
5 Who is the concert being sponsored by?
6 will it be shown on TV?
7 Will any famous people be invited to the concert?
8 How much money will be raised?

Units 1–6 Revision

A

1 Spanish isn't spoken here.
2 During this football match two players have been hurt so far./During this football match two players have hurt themselves so far.
3 The bus can't be driven without a special licence.
4 At the moment, the rules of the competition aren't being followed.
5 They helped each other to do the homework.
6 Megan and Tessa are always sending text messages to each other.
7 He fell from a tree and broke his leg.
8 I had a horrible week. I need to relax a bit.

There are no correct sentences.

B

1 help
2 you
3 be
4 all
5 by
6 make
7 Don't
8 by
9 been
10 has

C

Students' own translations:
1 They phone each other every day.
2 They weren't invited to the party.
3 A tiger has been seen in the centre of London.
4 The man is being followed by the police.
5 The new museum will be opened in 2017.
6 Rachel woke up very early this morning.
7 My finger hurts. I've cut myself!
8 We should have the invitations sent out immediately.

Exam skills 5–6

See www.oup.com/elt/teachersclub.

Unit 7

1

Across

4 go back to
6 look forward to
7 pick up
8 get over
9 put up with
10 grow out of
13 fall for
15 call for
16 get up

Down

1 pick on
2 get away
3 go out with
4 grow up
5 break up with
7 put away
10 get on with
11 fall over
12 look up to
14 wake up

2

1 up
2 up
3 away…after
4 out with
5 up with
6 up
7 for
8 away

3

1 You should stop picking on him!
2 I'm very tired. I'm looking forward to going on holiday.
3 The child has grown out of his car seat.
4 She and her sister have never got on well with each other.
5 She can't get over him.
6 His father is someone he looks up to.

4

2 When did she invite you
3 Did you reply
4 did you accept
5 aren't you going
6 What was in the second message
7 what do you want to do now
8 Would you like to come to the final with me

5

1 spend
2 like
3 went
4 (had) had
5 decided
6 goes
7 were

8 were opening
9 started
10 was
11 went
12 met
13 was
14 are going to go

6

1 Are you studying French?
2 How long have you been waiting for?
3 Are you going to see a movie/go to the cinema this evening/tonight?
4 How long have you known him?
5 How old will he be next year?
6 Where are you meeting Carolyn at eight o'clock?
7 When/What time does the train leave in the afternoon?
8 Where do you think people will live in a hundred years' time?

7

2 'm
3 was going
4 was getting
5 got
6 've never been
7 showed
8 has just asked
9 'm meeting
10 won't talk
11 has happened
12 'd wanted/wanted

8

1 get used to
2 get used to
3 are used to
4 used to
5 get used to
6 used to
7 was used to

9

1 used to run
2 are used
3 to walk
4 used to go
5 got used
6 I'm used to living
7 isn't used to getting
8 I used to go
9 get used to
10 use to like

10

1 got used to
2 am used/'ve got used
3 aren't used to
4 get used
5 are used
6 get used to

7 I'm used to
8 is used to
9 get used to
10 'm used to

11
2 gonna be @ sk%l l8r.
3 w%d u like 2 c me 2nite?
4 how r u doin?
5 gr8 thx.
6 call me b4 2moro.

Units 1–7 Revision

A
Students' own translations:
1 Emma and Jake get on very well. They said they would never break up.
2 I'm looking forward to leaving for the United States.
3 Can you turn off the lights, please? I'd like to go to sleep.
4 Where was this letter sent from?
5 Tomorrow's Dad's birthday and we haven't bought him anything yet.
6 When Dave arrived, we had already eaten.
7 When I was young, I used to have dinner at six.
8 I'm not used to being picked on.

B
1 long
2 used
3 got
4 Was
5 to
6 –
7 like
8 to
9 on
10 makes

C
Students' own translations:
1 He's fallen for an American girl.
2 Lois gets on with her parents very well.
3 If she picked on me again, I would tell my teacher.
4 Why should I put up with the noise from your MP3 player?
5 I know I should but I'll never get over him.
6 We're looking forward to going on holiday.
7 Are you getting used to living by yourself?
8 We used to spend Christmas Day at my grandmother's.

Unit 8

1
1 get
2 share/buy/rent
3 be
4 study/live
5 settle
6 have
7 apply for
8 leave
Students' own answers.

2
1 had finished…would have watched
2 hadn't worked…wouldn't have learnt
3 would have gone…hadn't lost
4 had phoned…would have met
5 had driven…wouldn't have had
6 would have made…hadn't died

3
Students' own answers.

4
2 He wouldn't have gone to Kendal if it hadn't rained.
3 If he hadn't looked at some jeans, he wouldn't have met Ellie.
4 If they hadn't gone to a café, Ellie wouldn't have lost her wallet.
5 He wouldn't have had to lend her some money if she hadn't lost her wallet.
6 If he hadn't lent her some money, they wouldn't have met next day.
7 If the weather hadn't been better, they wouldn't have gone for a walk.
8 He wouldn't have been able to text Ellie if he hadn't asked her for her phone number.

5
1 wouldn't
2 enjoy
3 hadn't won
4 'll come
5 'll stay
6 would
7 can
8 couldn't

6
1 g 2 f 3 e 4 a 5 c 6 b 7 h 8 d

7
1 If you don't finish your homework, you won't go out with your friends.
2 If I won the lottery, I would buy a yacht.
3 If Martin hadn't scored a goal, his team wouldn't have won the football match.
4 If Shakespeare hadn't been born there, Stratford-upon-Avon wouldn't be famous all over the world.
5 If he had got good exam results, he could have gone to the university.
6 If you are late home, your dad will be really angry with you.
7 If you go abroad next year, you will need to take your passport.
8 If I had a driving licence, I could drive a car.

8

Students' own translations:

1 If you turned down the music, I could study!
2 If I didn't have to study so much, I would be happier.
3 As soon as it stops raining, we'll go jogging.
4 If my father had lent me the car, we could have gone to the mountains.
5 If you stay in England for three months, your English will get better.
6 If I were rich, I would travel all year.
7 If I find your mobile, I'll take it to the reception desk.
8 If he hasn't got lost, he wouldn't have arrived late.

9

1 I had found a holiday job
2 we had met while we were in Madrid
3 she hadn't fallen off her bicycle
4 you hadn't eaten all the strawberries
5 I had learned to speak Spanish
6 she had told him the truth
7 I hadn't had a row with my parents
8 they had done their homework on time

10

1 wishes he hadn't missed
2 She wishes she had studied
3 They wish they hadn't gone
4 He wishes he had gone
5 They wish they had got

11

Students' own answers.

Units 1–8 Revision

A

1 would have
2 had taken
3 were
4 would
5 finish
6 had
7 could
8 had

B

1 Did, go out
2 went
3 had known
4 had told
5 could have come
6 would have enjoyed
7 hadn't talked/hadn't been talking
8 couldn't hear
9 made
10 don't, come

C

Students' own translations:

Sophie I'm really disappointed about the result of the competition.
Rebecca Really? But you did very well, didn't you? You nearly won it!
Sophie But if I'd written a better article, I'd have come first. I wish I hadn't come to the UK now.
Rebecca But if you hadn't come to the UK, you wouldn't have met all these people.
Sophie Yes, but if I'd stayed in Canada, the newspaper would have given me a permanent job.
Rebecca But you're a very good journalist. If you go back to Canada, the newspaper will probably give you a job anyway.
Sophie I hope so. Well, I've got to go now. Bye, Rebecca.
Rebecca Bye, Sophie. Good luck!

Exam skills 7–8

See www.oup.com/elt/teachersclub.

Self- check • Unit 1 to Unit 4

Read the descriptions in the table. Think about your progress and tick ✓ the column that is true for you.

* I'm not sure I can do this.   ** I can do this with some help.   *** I can do this easily.

In English I can …		*	**	***
Listening				
A2/B1	… understand essential information and the main points in everyday conversations (pp.10, 17, 19, 30, 40)			
B1	… follow the main points of a longer discussion (p.7)			
B1	… understand the main points in recorded material on topics of personal interest (pp.9, 13, 23, 42)			
B2	… identify speakers' attitudes in extended discussion on familiar topics (p.33)			
Reading				
B1	… understand the main points in short newspaper articles (pp.10, 12)			
B1	… skim texts to find relevant facts and information (p.32)			
B1	… understand those parts in private written texts dealing with events, feelings and wishes (p.38)			
B1	… guess the meaning of unknown words from the context (pp.13, 23, 33, 39, 42)			
B2	… read and understand longer articles and reports (pp.22, 32, 42)			
Speaking				
A2	… describe people and things (p.13)			
B1	… give or respond to advice on personal matters (pp.19, 20)			
B1	… start and maintain a conversation (p.37)			
B2	… speculate about hypothetical situations (pp.27, 29) or a likely chain of events (p.39)			
B2	… express different degrees of emotions (p.30)			
Writing				
A2/B1	… write texts about aspects of my everyday life: giving personal advice (p.23)			
A2/B1	… write a personal profile (p.43)			
B1	… write a detailed summary of a text I have read (p.33)			
B1	… write connected texts on topics of personal interest: favourite actors (p.13)			

Self- check • Unit 5 to Unit 8

Read the descriptions in the table. Think about your progress and tick ✓ the column that is true for you.

* I'm not sure I can do this.　　** I can do this with some help.　　*** I can do this easily.

In English I can ...		*	**	***
A2/B1	... understand and identify key points in news bulletins (p.59)			
A2/B1	... understand essential information and the main points in everyday conversations (pp.50, 60, 70)			
B1	... understand the plot of a story (p.80)			
B1	... follow the main points of an extended discussion (pp.53, 63, 73) or public speech (p.83)			
Reading				
B1	... guess the meaning of unknown words from the context (pp.53, 62, 72, 82)			
B1	... skim texts to find relevant facts and information (p.62)			
B1	... understand those parts in private written texts dealing with events, feelings and wishes (p.66)			
B1	... identify the writer's attitude towards the topic (p.72)			
B2	... read and understand longer articles and reports (pp.52, 62)			
B2	... understand articles on current problems in which the writers express specific points of view (pp.56, 82)			
Speaking				
B1	... give or ask for personal views and opinions in an informal discussion (pp.52, 72)			
B1/B2	... talk about advantages and disadvantages of a familiar subject (p.73)			
B2	... speculate about hypothetical situations (pp.47, 49, 63, 77, 79)			
B2	... construct a chain of logical arguments to deliver a speech on a given topic (p.73)			
Writing				
B1/B2	... write a news bulletin (p.59)			
B1	... write a formal letter on a topic of personal interest (p.63)			
B2	... summarise information from a recording (p.73)			
B2	... write a story about events and real or fictional experiences (pp.53, 83)			
B2	... write an argumentative essay on a familiar topic (p.73)			